100 THIRD GRADE SKILLS

Thinking Kids®
Carson-Dellosa Publishing LLC
Greensboro, North Carolina

Thinking Kids®
Carson-Dellosa Publishing LLC
P.O. Box 35665
Greensboro, NC 27425 USA

ISBN 978-1-4838-3118-3

Table of Contents

Table of Contents

50
MATH
SKILLS

Skill 1: Adding Through 20

addend   3 ⟶ Find the **3**-row.

addend   + 8 ⟶ Find the **8**-column.

sum   11 ⟵ The sum is named where the 3-row and the 8-column meet.

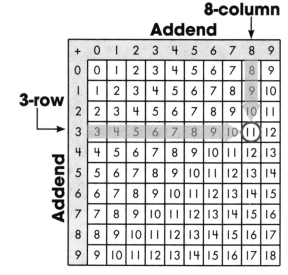

Directions: Add.

2 + 3 **5**	9 + 6	2 + 5	1 + 6	0 + 3
9 + 5	7 + 2	4 + 4	8 + 0	6 + 5
0 + 7	8 + 5	3 + 5	2 + 9	8 + 8
5 + 6	5 + 9	0 + 6	9 + 7	4 + 5

Skill 1: Adding Through 20

Directions: Add.

0 + 0	7 + 3	8 + 6	7 + 1
5 + 3	4 + 8	4 + 3	3 + 1
4 + 7	8 + 2	7 + 7	3 + 6
10 + 10	15 + 0	13 + 7	6 + 9
9 + 9	5 + 7	13 + 6	10 + 8

MATH

7-column

	0	1	2	3	4	5	6	7	8	9
0	0	1	2	3	4	5	6	7	8	9
1	1	2	3	4	5	6	7	8	9	10
2	2	3	4	5	6	7	8	9	10	11
3	3	4	5	6	7	8	9	10	11	12
4	4	5	6	7	8	9	10	11	12	13
5	5	6	7	8	9	10	11	12	13	14
6	6	7	8	9	10	11	12	13	14	15
7	7	8	9	10	11	12	13	14	15	16
8	8	9	10	11	12	13	14	15	16	17
9	9	10	11	12	13	14	15	16	17	18

minuend   1 2 ⟶ Find the **12** in the **7**-column.

subtrahend   – 7 ⟶

difference   5 ⟵ The difference is the number at the end of the row.

Directions: Subtract.

$$\begin{array}{r} 7 \\ -\ 2 \\ \hline 5 \end{array}$$

$$\begin{array}{r} 4 \\ -\ 0 \\ \hline \end{array}$$

$$\begin{array}{r} 5 \\ -\ 4 \\ \hline \end{array}$$

$$\begin{array}{r} 1\ 2 \\ -\ 6 \\ \hline \end{array}$$

$$\begin{array}{r} 1\ 6 \\ -\ 9 \\ \hline \end{array}$$

$$\begin{array}{r} 1\ 3 \\ -\ 8 \\ \hline \end{array}$$

$$\begin{array}{r} 6 \\ -\ 3 \\ \hline \end{array}$$

$$\begin{array}{r} 9 \\ -\ 6 \\ \hline \end{array}$$

$$\begin{array}{r} 5 \\ -\ 2 \\ \hline \end{array}$$

$$\begin{array}{r} 7 \\ -\ 0 \\ \hline \end{array}$$

$$\begin{array}{r} 1\ 8 \\ -\ 9 \\ \hline \end{array}$$

$$\begin{array}{r} 8 \\ -\ 7 \\ \hline \end{array}$$

$$\begin{array}{r} 6 \\ -\ 3 \\ \hline \end{array}$$

$$\begin{array}{r} 3 \\ -\ 0 \\ \hline \end{array}$$

$$\begin{array}{r} 8 \\ -\ 2 \\ \hline \end{array}$$

$$\begin{array}{r} 7 \\ -\ 4 \\ \hline \end{array}$$

$$\begin{array}{r} 1\ 0 \\ -\ 3 \\ \hline \end{array}$$

$$\begin{array}{r} 9 \\ -\ 2 \\ \hline \end{array}$$

$$\begin{array}{r} 1\ 7 \\ -\ 9 \\ \hline \end{array}$$

$$\begin{array}{r} 1\ 1 \\ -\ 3 \\ \hline \end{array}$$

MATH

Directions: Subtract.

13	3	19	13
- 3	- 2	- 4	- 5

13	17	12	6
- 8	- 4	- 5	- 4

1	12	10	11
- 0	- 3	- 5	- 5

3	20	9	5
- 1	- 3	- 1	- 1

8	14	10	20
- 7	- 8	- 1	- 9

MATH

3: Adding 2-Digit Numbers
(No Renaming)

First, add the ones.   Then, add the tens.

```
   4 3          4 3              4 3   addend  |    2 2   addend
 + 2 2        + 2 2            + 2 2   addend  |  + 1 6   addend
 ─────        ─────            ─────           |  ─────
                  5              6 5   sum     |    3 8   sum
```

- - - First, add the ones.
- - - Then, add the tens.

Directions: Add.

```
     2 3          2 2          2 0          1 5          7 3
   + 1 6        + 3 3        + 1 0        + 1 1        + 1 5
   ─────        ─────        ─────        ─────        ─────
     3 9
```

```
     6 3          1 0          1 8          1 3          3 3
   + 1 3        + 1 6        + 3 0        + 1 4        + 4 1
   ─────        ─────        ─────        ─────        ─────
```

```
     8 1          3 4          1 4          4 3          4 1
   + 1 1        + 2 1        + 1 2        + 1 2        + 1 8
   ─────        ─────        ─────        ─────        ─────
```

```
     4 0          2 7          2 2          5 4          3 6
   + 3 0        + 5 0        + 2 2        + 3 4        + 1 3
   ─────        ─────        ─────        ─────        ─────
```

MATH

Directions: Add.

17 + 51	13 + 42	12 + 44	32 + 16
27 + 42	31 + 38	13 + 14	15 + 44
23 + 42	22 + 71	36 + 50	35 + 23
10 + 43	73 + 20	86 + 13	52 + 13
42 + 26	32 + 45	61 + 31	25 + 24

MATH

11

4: Subtracting 2-Digit Numbers (No Renaming)

First, subtract the ones.　　　Then, subtract the tens.

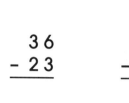

```
  3 6          3 6              3 6     minuend
- 2 3        - 2 3            - 2 3     subtrahend
              ─────            ─────
                  3            1 3      difference
```

Directions: Subtract.

```
    2 3          7 6          9 3          3 0          9 2
  - 1 2        - 2 2        - 7 1        - 1 0        - 1 1
  ─────        ─────        ─────        ─────        ─────
    1 5
```

```
    4 8          6 2          8 3          6 5          3 3
  - 1 6        - 1 0        - 1 3        - 4 4        - 1 2
  ─────        ─────        ─────        ─────        ─────
```

```
    3 7          8 8          8 6          8 2          8 9
  - 2 5        - 3 2        - 4 5        - 7 0        - 6 2
  ─────        ─────        ─────        ─────        ─────
```

```
    7 5          7 7          9 0          7 4          9 6
  - 6 2        - 4 4        - 6 0        - 2 2        - 5 3
  ─────        ─────        ─────        ─────        ─────
```

Skill 4: Subtracting 2-Digit Numbers (No Renaming)

Directions: Subtract.

$$\begin{array}{r} 82 \\ -\ 41 \\ \hline \end{array} \qquad \begin{array}{r} 47 \\ -\ 36 \\ \hline \end{array} \qquad \begin{array}{r} 35 \\ -\ 23 \\ \hline \end{array} \qquad \begin{array}{r} 66 \\ -\ 43 \\ \hline \end{array}$$

$$\begin{array}{r} 81 \\ -\ 60 \\ \hline \end{array} \qquad \begin{array}{r} 42 \\ -\ 30 \\ \hline \end{array} \qquad \begin{array}{r} 50 \\ -\ 30 \\ \hline \end{array} \qquad \begin{array}{r} 46 \\ -\ 25 \\ \hline \end{array}$$

$$\begin{array}{r} 92 \\ -\ 81 \\ \hline \end{array} \qquad \begin{array}{r} 75 \\ -\ 32 \\ \hline \end{array} \qquad \begin{array}{r} 57 \\ -\ 36 \\ \hline \end{array} \qquad \begin{array}{r} 29 \\ -\ 13 \\ \hline \end{array}$$

$$\begin{array}{r} 25 \\ -\ 15 \\ \hline \end{array} \qquad \begin{array}{r} 28 \\ -\ 12 \\ \hline \end{array} \qquad \begin{array}{r} 46 \\ -\ 13 \\ \hline \end{array} \qquad \begin{array}{r} 46 \\ -\ 15 \\ \hline \end{array}$$

$$\begin{array}{r} 75 \\ -\ 14 \\ \hline \end{array} \qquad \begin{array}{r} 64 \\ -\ 23 \\ \hline \end{array} \qquad \begin{array}{r} 59 \\ -\ 45 \\ \hline \end{array} \qquad \begin{array}{r} 83 \\ -\ 11 \\ \hline \end{array}$$

MATH

Adding 2-Digit Numbers (No Renaming)

Add the ones.
Rename 12 as 10 + 2.

Add the tens.

```
   37          7             37          37   addend
 + 25        + 5           + 25        + 25   addend
            ────           ────        ────
            12 or 10 + 2      2          62   sum
```

Directions: Add.

```
   23          76          14          36          18
 + 18        + 15        + 77        + 16        + 62
 ────
   41
```

```
   29          27          42          36          17
 + 19        + 36        + 39        + 28        + 16
```

```
   56          59          54          33          28
 + 27        + 13        + 27        + 28        + 17
```

```
   13          49          56          68          37
 + 19        + 17        + 14        + 23        + 46
```

Skill 5: Adding 2-Digit Numbers (No Renaming)

Directions: Add.

$$\begin{array}{r} 36 \\ +19 \\ \hline \end{array}\qquad \begin{array}{r} 27 \\ +18 \\ \hline \end{array}\qquad \begin{array}{r} 26 \\ +38 \\ \hline \end{array}\qquad \begin{array}{r} 18 \\ +13 \\ \hline \end{array}$$

$$\begin{array}{r} 72 \\ +18 \\ \hline \end{array}\qquad \begin{array}{r} 37 \\ +17 \\ \hline \end{array}\qquad \begin{array}{r} 23 \\ +57 \\ \hline \end{array}\qquad \begin{array}{r} 39 \\ +16 \\ \hline \end{array}$$

$$\begin{array}{r} 25 \\ +16 \\ \hline \end{array}\qquad \begin{array}{r} 28 \\ +14 \\ \hline \end{array}\qquad \begin{array}{r} 26 \\ +28 \\ \hline \end{array}\qquad \begin{array}{r} 76 \\ +15 \\ \hline \end{array}$$

$$\begin{array}{r} 29 \\ +17 \\ \hline \end{array}\qquad \begin{array}{r} 45 \\ +27 \\ \hline \end{array}\qquad \begin{array}{r} 43 \\ +27 \\ \hline \end{array}\qquad \begin{array}{r} 27 \\ +26 \\ \hline \end{array}$$

$$\begin{array}{r} 48 \\ +12 \\ \hline \end{array}\qquad \begin{array}{r} 45 \\ +46 \\ \hline \end{array}\qquad \begin{array}{r} 19 \\ +39 \\ \hline \end{array}\qquad \begin{array}{r} 51 \\ +19 \\ \hline \end{array}$$

MATH

Subtracting 2-Digit Numbers (No Renaming)

Subtract the ones. Rename 52 as "4 tens and 12 ones."	Subtract the ones.	Subtract the tens.	
$\begin{array}{r} 52 \\ -19 \\ \hline \end{array}$	$\begin{array}{r} {}^{4\ 12} \\ \cancel{5}\cancel{2} \\ -19 \\ \hline \end{array}$	$\begin{array}{r} {}^{4\ 12} \\ \cancel{5}\cancel{2} \\ -19 \\ \hline 3 \end{array}$	$\begin{array}{r} {}^{4\ 12} \\ \cancel{5}\cancel{2} \\ -19 \\ \hline 33 \end{array}$ minuend subtrahend difference

Directions: Subtract.

$\begin{array}{r} 30 \\ -22 \\ \hline 8 \end{array}$	$\begin{array}{r} 22 \\ -19 \\ \hline \end{array}$	$\begin{array}{r} 43 \\ -28 \\ \hline \end{array}$	$\begin{array}{r} 41 \\ -27 \\ \hline \end{array}$	$\begin{array}{r} 82 \\ -56 \\ \hline \end{array}$
$\begin{array}{r} 86 \\ -27 \\ \hline \end{array}$	$\begin{array}{r} 83 \\ -66 \\ \hline \end{array}$	$\begin{array}{r} 61 \\ -56 \\ \hline \end{array}$	$\begin{array}{r} 51 \\ -17 \\ \hline \end{array}$	$\begin{array}{r} 33 \\ -15 \\ \hline \end{array}$
$\begin{array}{r} 46 \\ -29 \\ \hline \end{array}$	$\begin{array}{r} 57 \\ -38 \\ \hline \end{array}$	$\begin{array}{r} 72 \\ -37 \\ \hline \end{array}$	$\begin{array}{r} 72 \\ -67 \\ \hline \end{array}$	$\begin{array}{r} 64 \\ -18 \\ \hline \end{array}$
$\begin{array}{r} 76 \\ -57 \\ \hline \end{array}$	$\begin{array}{r} 41 \\ -16 \\ \hline \end{array}$	$\begin{array}{r} 53 \\ -29 \\ \hline \end{array}$	$\begin{array}{r} 65 \\ -46 \\ \hline \end{array}$	$\begin{array}{r} 97 \\ -79 \\ \hline \end{array}$

6: Subtracting 2-Digit Numbers (No Renaming)

Directions: Subtract.

24 − 17	50 − 20	86 − 27	83 −26
52 −17	47 − 28	86 − 38	45 − 18
41 − 19	96 − 39	63 − 27	87 − 68
53 − 17	92 − 45	86 − 18	72 − 17
63 − 45	52 − 13	81 − 48	34 − 26

MATH

Skill 7: Adding Three Numbers

Add the ones.

$$
\begin{array}{r} 23 \\ 47 \\ +\ 16 \\ \hline \end{array}
$$

$$
\begin{array}{r} 3 \\ 7 \\ +\ 6 \\ \hline \end{array}
\quad 10
$$

$$
\begin{array}{r} 10 \\ +\ 6 \\ \hline 16 \end{array}
\text{ or } 10 + 6
$$

$$
\begin{array}{r} 1 \\ 23 \\ 47 \\ +\ 16 \\ \hline 6 \end{array}
$$

Add the tens.

$$
\begin{array}{r} 1 \\ 23 \\ 47 \\ +\ 16 \\ \hline 86 \end{array}
\begin{array}{l} \text{addend} \\ \text{addend} \\ \text{addend} \\ \text{sum} \end{array}
$$

Directions: Add.

$\begin{array}{r} 13 \\ 26 \\ +\ 45 \\ \hline 84 \end{array}$	$\begin{array}{r} 6 \\ 29 \\ +\ 43 \\ \hline \end{array}$	$\begin{array}{r} 16 \\ 23 \\ +\ 25 \\ \hline \end{array}$	$\begin{array}{r} 28 \\ 7 \\ +\ 33 \\ \hline \end{array}$	$\begin{array}{r} 6 \\ 13 \\ +\ 29 \\ \hline \end{array}$
$\begin{array}{r} 10 \\ 30 \\ +\ 50 \\ \hline \end{array}$	$\begin{array}{r} 22 \\ 31 \\ +\ 45 \\ \hline \end{array}$	$\begin{array}{r} 18 \\ 21 \\ +\ 33 \\ \hline \end{array}$	$\begin{array}{r} 29 \\ 16 \\ +\ 15 \\ \hline \end{array}$	$\begin{array}{r} 13 \\ 15 \\ +\ 25 \\ \hline \end{array}$
$\begin{array}{r} 41 \\ 21 \\ +\ 8 \\ \hline \end{array}$	$\begin{array}{r} 26 \\ 23 \\ +\ 35 \\ \hline \end{array}$	$\begin{array}{r} 11 \\ 30 \\ +\ 42 \\ \hline \end{array}$	$\begin{array}{r} 27 \\ 16 \\ +\ 8 \\ \hline \end{array}$	$\begin{array}{r} 4 \\ 7 \\ +\ 8 \\ \hline \end{array}$

MATH

Directions: Add.

```
   3 4          1 6          2 9          8 1
   1 6          2 3          3 1            5
 + 4 1        + 3 5        + 2 5        +   6


   3 3          7 6          1 8          4 1
   4 7            5          3 2          2 9
 + 1 2        +   3        + 1 6        + 1 6


   5 3          6 6          4 7          2 2
   2 1          2 1          1 4          4 1
 + 1 5        +   8        +   8        + 2 8


   2 3          1 8          2 3          6 4
   1 3          1 6          3 5          2 7
 + 1 7        + 2 4        + 1 7        +   4
```

MATH

8: Subtracting 2 Digits From 3 Digits

Subtract the ones.	To subtract the tens, rename the 1 hundred and 2 tens as "12 tens."	Subtract the tens.	

$$\begin{array}{r} 125 \\ -\ 84 \\ \hline \end{array} \qquad \begin{array}{r} 125 \\ -\ 84 \\ \hline 1 \end{array} \qquad \begin{array}{r} \overset{12}{\cancel{1}2 5} \\ -\ 84 \\ \hline 1 \end{array} \qquad \begin{array}{r} \overset{12}{\cancel{1}2 5} \\ -\ 84 \\ \hline 41 \end{array}$$

minuend
subtrahend

difference

Directions: Subtract.

$$\begin{array}{r} 173 \\ -\ 33 \\ \hline 140 \end{array} \qquad \begin{array}{r} 121 \\ -\ 60 \\ \hline \end{array} \qquad \begin{array}{r} 195 \\ -\ 44 \\ \hline \end{array} \qquad \begin{array}{r} 122 \\ -\ 11 \\ \hline \end{array} \qquad \begin{array}{r} 147 \\ -\ 53 \\ \hline \end{array}$$

$$\begin{array}{r} 182 \\ -\ 90 \\ \hline \end{array} \qquad \begin{array}{r} 143 \\ -\ 62 \\ \hline \end{array} \qquad \begin{array}{r} 180 \\ -\ 70 \\ \hline \end{array} \qquad \begin{array}{r} 119 \\ -\ 15 \\ \hline \end{array} \qquad \begin{array}{r} 123 \\ -\ 12 \\ \hline \end{array}$$

$$\begin{array}{r} 186 \\ -\ 65 \\ \hline \end{array} \qquad \begin{array}{r} 187 \\ -\ 42 \\ \hline \end{array} \qquad \begin{array}{r} 154 \\ -\ 13 \\ \hline \end{array} \qquad \begin{array}{r} 127 \\ -\ 83 \\ \hline \end{array} \qquad \begin{array}{r} 187 \\ -\ 67 \\ \hline \end{array}$$

$$\begin{array}{r} 135 \\ -\ 42 \\ \hline \end{array} \qquad \begin{array}{r} 115 \\ -\ 24 \\ \hline \end{array} \qquad \begin{array}{r} 171 \\ -\ 60 \\ \hline \end{array} \qquad \begin{array}{r} 148 \\ -\ 56 \\ \hline \end{array} \qquad \begin{array}{r} 191 \\ -\ 77 \\ \hline \end{array}$$

Directions: Subtract.

$$\begin{array}{r} 132 \\ -51 \\ \hline \end{array}$$
$$\begin{array}{r} 177 \\ -43 \\ \hline \end{array}$$
$$\begin{array}{r} 192 \\ -71 \\ \hline \end{array}$$
$$\begin{array}{r} 186 \\ -92 \\ \hline \end{array}$$

$$\begin{array}{r} 134 \\ -72 \\ \hline \end{array}$$
$$\begin{array}{r} 125 \\ -45 \\ \hline \end{array}$$
$$\begin{array}{r} 129 \\ -86 \\ \hline \end{array}$$
$$\begin{array}{r} 176 \\ -75 \\ \hline \end{array}$$

$$\begin{array}{r} 120 \\ -40 \\ \hline \end{array}$$
$$\begin{array}{r} 194 \\ -53 \\ \hline \end{array}$$
$$\begin{array}{r} 189 \\ -62 \\ \hline \end{array}$$
$$\begin{array}{r} 134 \\ -42 \\ \hline \end{array}$$

$$\begin{array}{r} 165 \\ -51 \\ \hline \end{array}$$
$$\begin{array}{r} 167 \\ -45 \\ \hline \end{array}$$
$$\begin{array}{r} 150 \\ -30 \\ \hline \end{array}$$
$$\begin{array}{r} 157 \\ -63 \\ \hline \end{array}$$

$$\begin{array}{r} 149 \\ -61 \\ \hline \end{array}$$
$$\begin{array}{r} 139 \\ -62 \\ \hline \end{array}$$
$$\begin{array}{r} 175 \\ -82 \\ \hline \end{array}$$
$$\begin{array}{r} 167 \\ -43 \\ \hline \end{array}$$

$$\begin{array}{r} 133 \\ -41 \\ \hline \end{array}$$
$$\begin{array}{r} 148 \\ -78 \\ \hline \end{array}$$
$$\begin{array}{r} 165 \\ -43 \\ \hline \end{array}$$
$$\begin{array}{r} 128 \\ -57 \\ \hline \end{array}$$

9: Adding 3-Digit Numbers

	Add the ones.	Add the tens.	Add the hundreds.
	$\overset{1}{}$	$\overset{1\,1}{}$	$\overset{1\,1}{}$
755	755	755	755
+ 469	+ 469	+ 469	+ 469
	4	24	1224

Directions: Add.

```
   123        982        342        782        123
 + 562      + 171      + 591      + 341      + 321
 ─────      ─────      ─────      ─────      ─────
   685
```

```
   681        862        900        720        931
 + 975      + 313      + 130      + 850      + 111
 ─────      ─────      ─────      ─────      ─────
```

```
   823        547        861        862        431
 + 457      + 321      + 421      + 139      + 250
 ─────      ─────      ─────      ─────      ─────
```

```
   782        751        871        337        606
 + 191      + 605      + 323      + 488      + 222
 ─────      ─────      ─────      ─────      ─────
```

Skill 9: Adding 3-Digit Numbers

Directions: Add.

791 + 191	144 + 800	192 + 175	257 + 147
203 + 211	541 + 693	705 + 719	641 + 209
873 + 505	700 + 650	105 + 341	450 + 362
593 + 741	861 + 209	735 + 145	820 + 431
738 + 387	719 + 120	153 + 312	712 + 210
619 + 715	205 + 316	153 + 814	613 + 261

MATH

10: Subtracting 3-Digit Numbers

Rename 2 tens and 1 one as "1 ten and 11 ones." Then, subtract the ones.

Rename 6 hundreds and 1 ten as "5 hundreds and 11 tens." Then, subtract the tens.

Subtract the hundreds.

```
              1 11
  6 2 1     6 2̶ 1̶
- 2 5 9   - 2 5 9
            ─────────
                  2
```

```
    11
  5 2̶ 11
  6̶ 2̶ 1̶
- 2 5 9
─────────
    6 2
```

```
    11
  5 2̶ 11
  6̶ 2̶ 1̶       minuend
- 2 5 9       subtrahend
─────────
  3 6 2       difference
```

Directions: Subtract.

```
  3 2 1        7 4 5        6 3 9        8 3 0        6 2 6
- 1 0 9      - 1 5 2      - 1 5 0      - 7 1 0      - 1 4 6
─────────
  2 1 2
```

```
  4 5 7        7 2 9        6 5 7        3 8 6        4 1 1
- 3 0 9      - 3 2 1      - 4 5 1      - 1 0 7      - 3 0 5
```

```
  4 8 6        3 1 1        9 8 3        9 7 1        8 7 6
- 1 0 9      - 1 2 1      - 6 5 2      - 5 7 2      - 3 5 7
```

```
  5 4 9        7 2 1        9 5 8        6 4 4        9 0 9
- 3 6 0      - 1 4 4      - 6 3 7      - 4 2 8      - 8 7 5
```

Directions: Subtract.

$$
\begin{array}{r} 256 \\ -142 \\ \hline \end{array}
\qquad
\begin{array}{r} 347 \\ -139 \\ \hline \end{array}
\qquad
\begin{array}{r} 725 \\ -196 \\ \hline \end{array}
\qquad
\begin{array}{r} 863 \\ -692 \\ \hline \end{array}
$$

$$
\begin{array}{r} 980 \\ -532 \\ \hline \end{array}
\qquad
\begin{array}{r} 720 \\ -500 \\ \hline \end{array}
\qquad
\begin{array}{r} 543 \\ -457 \\ \hline \end{array}
\qquad
\begin{array}{r} 762 \\ -135 \\ \hline \end{array}
$$

$$
\begin{array}{r} 132 \\ -107 \\ \hline \end{array}
\qquad
\begin{array}{r} 921 \\ -571 \\ \hline \end{array}
\qquad
\begin{array}{r} 631 \\ -545 \\ \hline \end{array}
\qquad
\begin{array}{r} 982 \\ -144 \\ \hline \end{array}
$$

$$
\begin{array}{r} 531 \\ -250 \\ \hline \end{array}
\qquad
\begin{array}{r} 720 \\ -371 \\ \hline \end{array}
\qquad
\begin{array}{r} 582 \\ -357 \\ \hline \end{array}
\qquad
\begin{array}{r} 793 \\ -457 \\ \hline \end{array}
$$

$$
\begin{array}{r} 612 \\ -483 \\ \hline \end{array}
\qquad
\begin{array}{r} 592 \\ -107 \\ \hline \end{array}
\qquad
\begin{array}{r} 343 \\ -240 \\ \hline \end{array}
\qquad
\begin{array}{r} 916 \\ -532 \\ \hline \end{array}
$$

MATH

Thinking Subtraction for Addition

To check

215 + 109 = 324,

subtract 109 from 324.

$$
\begin{array}{r}
2\ 1\ 5 \\
+\ 1\ 0\ 9 \\
\hline
3\ 2\ 4 \\
-\ 1\ 0\ 9 \\
\hline
2\ 1\ 5
\end{array}
$$

These should be the same.

Directions: Add. Check each answer.

$$
\begin{array}{r}
1\ 5\ 7 \\
+\ 2\ 1\ 2 \\
\hline
3\ 6\ 9 \\
-\ 2\ 1\ 2 \\
\hline
1\ 5\ 7
\end{array}
$$

$$
\begin{array}{r}
7\ 1\ 9 \\
+\ 1\ 8\ 2 \\
\hline
\end{array}
$$

$$
\begin{array}{r}
3\ 1\ 2 \\
+\ 1\ 0\ 5 \\
\hline
\end{array}
$$

$$
\begin{array}{r}
3\ 1\ 3 \\
+\ 6\ 1\ 9 \\
\hline
\end{array}
$$

$$
\begin{array}{r}
3\ 0\ 6 \\
+\ 2\ 1\ 5 \\
\hline
\end{array}
$$

$$
\begin{array}{r}
1\ 2\ 0 \\
+\ 1\ 7\ 0 \\
\hline
\end{array}
$$

$$
\begin{array}{r}
7\ 1\ 0 \\
+\ 3\ 9\ 8 \\
\hline
\end{array}
$$

$$
\begin{array}{r}
4\ 5\ 7 \\
+\ 3\ 4\ 9 \\
\hline
\end{array}
$$

$$
\begin{array}{r}
7\ 1\ 2 \\
+\ 3\ 6\ 3 \\
\hline
\end{array}
$$

$$
\begin{array}{r}
7\ 1\ 4 \\
+\ 2\ 9\ 1 \\
\hline
\end{array}
$$

$$
\begin{array}{r}
3\ 1\ 1 \\
+\ \ \ 8\ 8 \\
\hline
\end{array}
$$

$$
\begin{array}{r}
4\ 1\ 9 \\
+\ \ \ 5\ 7 \\
\hline
\end{array}
$$

MATH

Skill **11**: Thinking Subtraction for Addition

Directions: Add. Check each answer.

$$\begin{array}{r} 400 \\ + 547 \\ \hline \end{array} \qquad \begin{array}{r} 591 \\ + 120 \\ \hline \end{array} \qquad \begin{array}{r} 612 \\ + 319 \\ \hline \end{array} \qquad \begin{array}{r} 325 \\ + 125 \\ \hline \end{array}$$

$$\begin{array}{r} 411 \\ + 120 \\ \hline \end{array} \qquad \begin{array}{r} 247 \\ + 259 \\ \hline \end{array} \qquad \begin{array}{r} 863 \\ + 192 \\ \hline \end{array} \qquad \begin{array}{r} 459 \\ + 130 \\ \hline \end{array}$$

$$\begin{array}{r} 303 \\ + 209 \\ \hline \end{array} \qquad \begin{array}{r} 711 \\ + 191 \\ \hline \end{array} \qquad \begin{array}{r} 252 \\ + 130 \\ \hline \end{array} \qquad \begin{array}{r} 411 \\ + 283 \\ \hline \end{array}$$

$$\begin{array}{r} 601 \\ + 176 \\ \hline \end{array} \qquad \begin{array}{r} 575 \\ + 251 \\ \hline \end{array} \qquad \begin{array}{r} 723 \\ + 197 \\ \hline \end{array} \qquad \begin{array}{r} 358 \\ + 492 \\ \hline \end{array}$$

MATH

Skill 12: Thinking Addition for Subtraction

To check

982 − 657 = 325,

add 657 to 325.

```
  982 ◄-----
- 657        ¦
  325        ¦   These should be the same.
+ 657        ¦
  982 ◄------
```

Directions: Subtract. Check each answer.

```
   720        321        126        983
-  150      -  83      -  92      - 657
   570
+  150
   720
```

```
   456        442        300        117
-  291      - 220      - 179      - 104
```

```
   423        259        638        708
-  197      - 147      - 463      - 412
```

Directions: Subtract. Check each answer.

519 − 120	640 − 320	192 − 86	710 − 441
683 − 419	712 − 307	719 − 532	919 − 457
731 − 250	912 − 609	542 − 327	728 − 530
939 − 482	766 − 149	819 − 640	643 − 391

MATH

13: Adding 3 or More Numbers (1- and 2-digit)

Add the ones.　　　　　　　　　　　　　　　　Add the tens.

$$
\begin{array}{r} 45 \\ 62 \\ +94 \\ \hline \end{array}
\qquad
\begin{array}{r} 5 \\ 2 \\ +4 \\ \hline \end{array}
\begin{array}{r} 7 \\ +4 \\ \hline 11 \end{array}
\text{ or } 10+1
\qquad
\begin{array}{r} 1 \\ 45 \\ 62 \\ +94 \\ \hline 1 \end{array}
\qquad
\begin{array}{r} 1 \\ 45 \\ 62 \\ +94 \\ \hline 201 \end{array}
$$

Directions: Add.

$$
\begin{array}{r} 3 \\ 6 \\ +9 \\ \hline 18 \end{array}
\qquad
\begin{array}{r} 7 \\ 5 \\ +8 \\ \hline \end{array}
\qquad
\begin{array}{r} 6 \\ 12 \\ +13 \\ \hline \end{array}
\qquad
\begin{array}{r} 8 \\ 17 \\ +19 \\ \hline \end{array}
\qquad
\begin{array}{r} 12 \\ 32 \\ +53 \\ \hline \end{array}
$$

$$
\begin{array}{r} 8 \\ 6 \\ +2 \\ \hline \end{array}
\qquad
\begin{array}{r} 17 \\ 93 \\ +23 \\ \hline \end{array}
\qquad
\begin{array}{r} 16 \\ 45 \\ +92 \\ \hline \end{array}
\qquad
\begin{array}{r} 82 \\ 18 \\ +23 \\ \hline \end{array}
\qquad
\begin{array}{r} 7 \\ 19 \\ +57 \\ \hline \end{array}
$$

$$
\begin{array}{r} 22 \\ 86 \\ +34 \\ \hline \end{array}
\qquad
\begin{array}{r} 50 \\ 40 \\ +60 \\ \hline \end{array}
\qquad
\begin{array}{r} 86 \\ 93 \\ +72 \\ \hline \end{array}
\qquad
\begin{array}{r} 23 \\ 35 \\ +62 \\ \hline \end{array}
\qquad
\begin{array}{r} 18 \\ 35 \\ +67 \\ \hline \end{array}
$$

Adding 3 or More Numbers (1- and 2-digit)

Directions: Add.

$$\begin{array}{r} 86 \\ 54 \\ + 83 \\ \hline \end{array}$$
$$\begin{array}{r} 32 \\ 49 \\ + 76 \\ \hline \end{array}$$
$$\begin{array}{r} 13 \\ 19 \\ + 23 \\ \hline \end{array}$$
$$\begin{array}{r} 25 \\ 66 \\ + 72 \\ \hline \end{array}$$

$$\begin{array}{r} 81 \\ 19 \\ + 83 \\ \hline \end{array}$$
$$\begin{array}{r} 53 \\ 42 \\ + 93 \\ \hline \end{array}$$
$$\begin{array}{r} 13 \\ 12 \\ + 14 \\ \hline \end{array}$$
$$\begin{array}{r} 10 \\ 20 \\ + 90 \\ \hline \end{array}$$

$$\begin{array}{r} 82 \\ 76 \\ + 54 \\ \hline \end{array}$$
$$\begin{array}{r} 86 \\ 54 \\ 32 \\ + 52 \\ \hline \end{array}$$
$$\begin{array}{r} 92 \\ 10 \\ 53 \\ + 47 \\ \hline \end{array}$$
$$\begin{array}{r} 81 \\ 71 \\ 36 \\ + 27 \\ \hline \end{array}$$

$$\begin{array}{r} 12 \\ 18 \\ 24 \\ + 19 \\ \hline \end{array}$$
$$\begin{array}{r} 93 \\ 48 \\ 13 \\ + 27 \\ \hline \end{array}$$
$$\begin{array}{r} 41 \\ 86 \\ 53 \\ + 22 \\ \hline \end{array}$$
$$\begin{array}{r} 63 \\ 49 \\ 18 \\ + 50 \\ \hline \end{array}$$

Adding 3 or More Numbers (3-digit)

	Add the ones.	Add the tens.	Add the hundreds.
231 457 + 625	231 457 + 625 3	231 457 + 625 13	231 457 + 625 1313

Directions: Add.

522 367 + 151 1,040	868 321 + 405	150 200 + 300	701 231 + 862	986 105 + 525
129 318 + 467	803 623 + 186	545 309 + 119	868 740 + 809	132 195 + 118
200 300 + 600	180 240 + 303	861 757 + 409	863 404 + 891	731 356 + 402

Skill 14: Adding 3 or More Numbers (3-digit)

Directions: Add.

$$
\begin{array}{r} 865 \\ 591 \\ +217 \\ \hline \end{array}
\qquad
\begin{array}{r} 238 \\ 405 \\ +596 \\ \hline \end{array}
\qquad
\begin{array}{r} 898 \\ 777 \\ +192 \\ \hline \end{array}
\qquad
\begin{array}{r} 341 \\ 127 \\ +192 \\ \hline \end{array}
$$

$$
\begin{array}{r} 864 \\ 425 \\ +323 \\ \hline \end{array}
\qquad
\begin{array}{r} 127 \\ 291 \\ +867 \\ \hline \end{array}
\qquad
\begin{array}{r} 205 \\ 876 \\ +198 \\ \hline \end{array}
\qquad
\begin{array}{r} 712 \\ 490 \\ +600 \\ \hline \end{array}
$$

$$
\begin{array}{r} 750 \\ 400 \\ +203 \\ \hline \end{array}
\qquad
\begin{array}{r} 591 \\ 603 \\ 907 \\ +432 \\ \hline \end{array}
\qquad
\begin{array}{r} 862 \\ 191 \\ 183 \\ +251 \\ \hline \end{array}
\qquad
\begin{array}{r} 892 \\ 645 \\ 320 \\ +123 \\ \hline \end{array}
$$

$$
\begin{array}{r} 132 \\ 169 \\ 119 \\ +105 \\ \hline \end{array}
\qquad
\begin{array}{r} 323 \\ 309 \\ 452 \\ +690 \\ \hline \end{array}
\qquad
\begin{array}{r} 712 \\ 613 \\ 518 \\ +437 \\ \hline \end{array}
\qquad
\begin{array}{r} 212 \\ 841 \\ 360 \\ +174 \\ \hline \end{array}
$$

MATH

Skill 15: Adding 4-Digit Numbers

	Add the ones.	Add the tens.	Add the hundreds.	Add the thousands.

3746	¹ 3746	¹¹ 3746	¹¹¹ 3746	¹¹¹ 3746
+ 5899	+ 5899	+ 5899	+ 5899	+ 5899
	5	45	645	9645

Directions: Add.

7865	8654	4320	3543	4293
+ 1192	+ 1219	+ 3069	+ 3921	+ 5176
9,057				

6405	1982	7083	4325	6057
+ 3398	+ 1782	+ 2907	+ 4986	+ 1239

8761	2305	3050	6932	5437
+ 1032	+ 5747	+ 4707	+ 2349	+ 2968

1718	7923	4523	5111	3597
+ 2347	+ 1250	+ 3962	+ 2699	+ 4922

MATH

Skill 15: Adding 4-Digit Numbers

Directions: Add.

5431 + 2989	7986 + 1479	1119 + 2459	7239 + 1635
2450 + 7267	6527 + 2985	5431 + 1982	7986 + 1246
1543 + 3989	7121 + 1923	8763 + 1005	4321 + 2387
5450 + 1987	4733 + 2576	3981 + 2877	6986 + 2928
7181 + 2111	7900 + 2005	6919 + 1255	2873 + 5464

MATH

Skill 16: Subtracting to 4 Digits

Subtract the ones.	Rename 4 hundreds and 3 tens as "3 hundreds and 13 tens." Subtract the tens.	Rename 5 thousands and 3 hundreds as "4 thousands and 13 hundreds." Subtract the hundreds.	Subtract the thousands.

$$\begin{array}{r} 5437 \\ -1592 \\ \hline \end{array}$$

$$\begin{array}{r} 5437 \\ -1592 \\ \hline 5 \end{array}$$

$$\begin{array}{r} \overset{3\ 13}{5\cancel{4}\cancel{3}7} \\ -1592 \\ \hline 45 \end{array}$$

$$\begin{array}{r} \overset{13}{\underset{}{4\ \cancel{3}\ 13}} \\ \cancel{5}\cancel{4}\cancel{3}7 \\ -1592 \\ \hline 845 \end{array}$$

$$\begin{array}{r} \overset{13}{\underset{}{4\ \cancel{3}\ 13}} \\ \cancel{5}\cancel{4}\cancel{3}7 \\ -1592 \\ \hline 3845 \end{array}$$

Directions: Subtract.

$$\begin{array}{r} 9865 \\ -2382 \\ \hline 7,483 \end{array} \qquad \begin{array}{r} 7528 \\ -792 \\ \hline \end{array} \qquad \begin{array}{r} 8654 \\ -3993 \\ \hline \end{array} \qquad \begin{array}{r} 1925 \\ -183 \\ \hline \end{array}$$

$$\begin{array}{r} 1876 \\ -982 \\ \hline \end{array} \qquad \begin{array}{r} 5473 \\ -3591 \\ \hline \end{array} \qquad \begin{array}{r} 8762 \\ -682 \\ \hline \end{array} \qquad \begin{array}{r} 7945 \\ -963 \\ \hline \end{array}$$

$$\begin{array}{r} 8654 \\ -772 \\ \hline \end{array} \qquad \begin{array}{r} 7846 \\ -3974 \\ \hline \end{array} \qquad \begin{array}{r} 6932 \\ -2840 \\ \hline \end{array} \qquad \begin{array}{r} 1389 \\ -794 \\ \hline \end{array}$$

$$\begin{array}{r} 2545 \\ -963 \\ \hline \end{array} \qquad \begin{array}{r} 7863 \\ -2572 \\ \hline \end{array} \qquad \begin{array}{r} 8121 \\ -640 \\ \hline \end{array} \qquad \begin{array}{r} 9043 \\ -2177 \\ \hline \end{array}$$

Directions: Subtract.

```
  7865          3456          7982
-  974        -  661        -  490
```

```
  8163          4325          9876
- 4670        - 1534        -  985
```

```
  8716          5432          3287
- 5823        - 3651        -  395
```

```
  7805          5439          4321
-  164        -  767        -  841
```

```
  7865          7976          5439
-  974        - 4682        -  866
```

MATH

Rounding numbers is a way of replacing one number with another number that tells about how many or how much.

When rounding to the nearest number, look at the digit to the right of it. If that column has 0, 1, 2, 3, or 4 in it, round down. If the column has 5, 6, 7, 8, or 9 in it, round up.

Round 23 to the nearest ten.
Look at the ones digit.

20   **23**   30

Round 23 down to 20.

Round 284 to the nearest hundred.
Look at the tens digit.

200   **284**   300

Round 284 up to 300.

Directions: Round the numbers to the place value listed.

ten		hundred	
23	_____	483	_____
567	_____	809	_____
775	_____	495	_____
2,813	_____	311	_____
408	_____	407	_____
742	_____	3,054	_____
384	_____	609	_____
99	_____	937	_____
826	_____	148	_____

Skill 17: Rounding

Directions: Draw an arrow to show which way to round the number to the nearest ten or hundred. Then, write the rounded number. The first one is done for you.

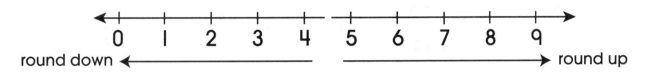

round down ← — — — — — — — — — — → round up

Ten

258	↑	260
722		
48		
391		
928		
53		
137		
558		

Hundred

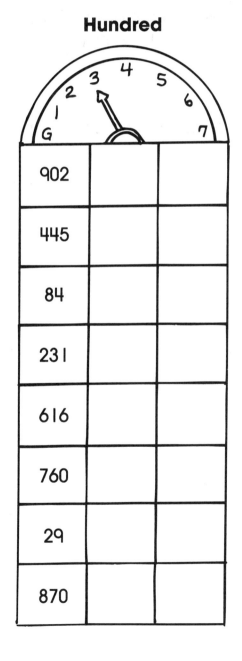

902		
445		
84		
231		
616		
760		
29		
870		

MATH

Skill 18: Estimating Addition

Round each number to the highest place value the numbers have in common. Then, add from right to left.

$$
\begin{array}{r}
194 \longrightarrow 190 \\
+\ 76 \longrightarrow +\ 80 \\
\hline
270
\end{array}
\qquad
\begin{array}{r}
203 \longrightarrow 200 \\
+\ 196 \longrightarrow +\ 200 \\
\hline
400
\end{array}
$$

The highest place value for 194 and 76 is the tens place. Round 194 and 76 to the tens place. Add.

The highest place value for 203 and 196 is the hundreds place. Round 203 and 196 to the hundreds place. Add.

Directions: Estimate each sum.

$$
\begin{array}{r}
25 \\
+\ 36 \\
\hline
\end{array}
\qquad
\begin{array}{r}
30 \\
+\ 40 \\
\hline
70
\end{array}
\qquad\qquad
\begin{array}{r}
23 \\
+\ 14 \\
\hline
\end{array}
\qquad\qquad
\begin{array}{r}
57 \\
+\ 51 \\
\hline
\end{array}
$$

$$
\begin{array}{r}
42 \\
+\ 92 \\
\hline
\end{array}
\qquad\qquad
\begin{array}{r}
92 \\
+\ 51 \\
\hline
\end{array}
\qquad\qquad
\begin{array}{r}
131 \\
+\ 42 \\
\hline
\end{array}
$$

$$
\begin{array}{r}
165 \\
+\ 92 \\
\hline
\end{array}
\qquad\qquad
\begin{array}{r}
147 \\
+\ 97 \\
\hline
\end{array}
\qquad\qquad
\begin{array}{r}
147 \\
+\ 362 \\
\hline
\end{array}
$$

Skill 18: Estimating Addition

Directions: Estimate each sum.

$$
\begin{array}{r}
175 \\
+\ 302 \\
\hline
\end{array}
\qquad
\begin{array}{r}
457 \\
+\ 603 \\
\hline
\end{array}
\qquad
\begin{array}{r}
543 \\
+\ 261 \\
\hline
\end{array}
$$

$$
\begin{array}{r}
1132 \\
+\ \ 432 \\
\hline
\end{array}
\qquad
\begin{array}{r}
1250 \\
+\ \ 347 \\
\hline
\end{array}
\qquad
\begin{array}{r}
5786 \\
+\ \ 432 \\
\hline
\end{array}
$$

$$
\begin{array}{r}
4679 \\
+\ \ 578 \\
\hline
\end{array}
\qquad
\begin{array}{r}
1562 \\
+\ 3492 \\
\hline
\end{array}
\qquad
\begin{array}{r}
6054 \\
+\ 6542 \\
\hline
\end{array}
$$

$$
\begin{array}{r}
3541 \\
+\ 7987 \\
\hline
\end{array}
\qquad
\begin{array}{r}
2795 \\
+\ 2454 \\
\hline
\end{array}
\qquad
\begin{array}{r}
5232 \\
+\ \ 651 \\
\hline
\end{array}
$$

MATH

Round each number to the highest place value the numbers have in common.

```
236  ⟶   240
- 49  ⟶  - 50
          190
```

```
396  ⟶   400
- 287 ⟶  - 300
           100
```

The highest place value for 236 and 49 is the tens place. Round 236 and 49 to the tens place. Subtract.

The highest place value for 396 and 287 is the hundreds place. Round 396 and 287 to the hundreds place. Subtract.

Directions: Estimate each difference.

```
  56     60
- 43   - 40
         20
```

```
  49
- 12
```

```
  72
- 61
```

```
  80
- 45
```

```
  451
-  72
```

```
  986
-  59
```

```
  760
-  32
```

```
  542
-  57
```

```
  543
- 290
```

MATH

Directions: Estimate each difference.

$$\begin{array}{r} 943 \\ -457 \\ \hline \end{array} \qquad \begin{array}{r} 547 \\ -249 \\ \hline \end{array} \qquad \begin{array}{r} 686 \\ -162 \\ \hline \end{array}$$

$$\begin{array}{r} 1543 \\ -661 \\ \hline \end{array} \qquad \begin{array}{r} 3247 \\ -843 \\ \hline \end{array} \qquad \begin{array}{r} 4560 \\ -493 \\ \hline \end{array}$$

$$\begin{array}{r} 7631 \\ -647 \\ \hline \end{array} \qquad \begin{array}{r} 8798 \\ -4453 \\ \hline \end{array} \qquad \begin{array}{r} 9476 \\ -2652 \\ \hline \end{array}$$

$$\begin{array}{r} 7345 \\ -6443 \\ \hline \end{array} \qquad \begin{array}{r} 9432 \\ -1486 \\ \hline \end{array} \qquad \begin{array}{r} 6849 \\ -3493 \\ \hline \end{array}$$

MATH

Skill 20: Understanding Multiplication

To multiply means to use repeated addition. Make equal groups and then add all of the groups together.

The answer to a multiplication problem is called the **product**. The numbers being multiplied are called **factors**.

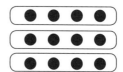

4 + 4 + 4
3 groups of 4
3 × 4 ← factors
12 ← product

Directions: Add. Then, multiply.

____ + ____ + ____ + ____ = ____

____ sets of ____ equals ____

____ × ____ = ____

____ + ____ + ____ = ____

____ sets of ____ equals ____

____ × ____ = ____

____ + ____ + ____ + ____

+ ____ = ____

____ sets of ____ equals ____

____ × ____ = ____

____ + ____ + ____ + ____ + ____

+ ____ = ____

____ sets of ____ equals ____

____ × ____ = ____

Skill 20: Understanding Multiplication

Directions: Write an addition and multiplication problem for each picture. Then, find the sum and the product.

× × × × × ×
 ×   ×   ×
× × × × × ×

☆ ☆   ☆ ☆
  ☆   ☆

□ + □ + □ = □

□ + □ = □

□ × □ = □

□ × □ = □

O   O   O   O
O   O   O   O

℮ ℮ ℮ ℮

℮ ℮ ℮ ℮

□ + □ + □ + □ = □

□ + □ = □

□ × □ = □

□ × □ = □

× × ×
× × ×
× × ×

☆☆ ☆☆ ☆☆
☆☆ ☆☆ ☆☆

□ + □ + □ = □

□ + □ + □ = □

□ × □ = □

□ × □ = □

Skill 21: Multiplying Through 5 × 5

factor   3 ⟶ Find the **3**-row.

factor   × 5 ⟶ Find the **5**-column.

product   1 5 ⟵ The product is named where the 3-row and the 5-column meet.

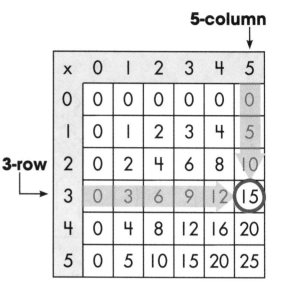

Directions: Multiply.

2	5	1	1
× 5	× 3	× 3	× 4
10			

3	5	0	1
× 4	× 2	× 5	× 1

3	2	0	4
× 5	× 2	× 3	× 3

MATH

Skill 21: Multiplying Through 5 × 5

Directions: Multiply.

4 × 4	5 × 2	4 × 5	2 × 3	5 × 5
5 × 0	4 × 2	0 × 0	3 × 3	4 × 4
3 × 2	1 × 2	0 × 2	3 × 3	2 × 4
4 × 0	3 × 2	5 × 4	5 × 1	2 × 0
3 × 1	5 × 5	1 × 0	2 × 4	3 × 0

MATH

22: Multiplying Through 5 × 9

factor   3 ⟶ Find the **3**-row.

factor   × 7 ⟶ Find the **7**-column.

product   2 1 ⟵ The product is named where the 3-row and the 5-column meet.

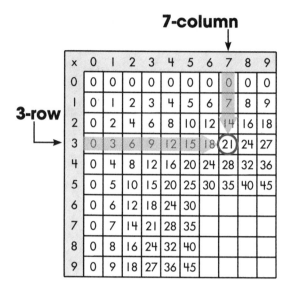

Directions: Multiply.

$$\begin{array}{r} 5 \\ \times\ 0 \\ \hline 0 \end{array} \qquad \begin{array}{r} 3 \\ \times\ 9 \\ \hline \end{array} \qquad \begin{array}{r} 6 \\ \times\ 5 \\ \hline \end{array} \qquad \begin{array}{r} 1 \\ \times\ 4 \\ \hline \end{array}$$

$$\begin{array}{r} 5 \\ \times\ 1 \\ \hline \end{array} \qquad \begin{array}{r} 6 \\ \times\ 3 \\ \hline \end{array} \qquad \begin{array}{r} 9 \\ \times\ 2 \\ \hline \end{array} \qquad \begin{array}{r} 8 \\ \times\ 5 \\ \hline \end{array}$$

$$\begin{array}{r} 5 \\ \times\ 8 \\ \hline \end{array} \qquad \begin{array}{r} 0 \\ \times\ 0 \\ \hline \end{array} \qquad \begin{array}{r} 2 \\ \times\ 9 \\ \hline \end{array} \qquad \begin{array}{r} 3 \\ \times\ 4 \\ \hline \end{array}$$

Skill 22: Multiplying Through 5 × 9

Directions: Multiply.

4 × 6	7 × 3	6 × 1	7 × 2	3 × 5
4 × 1	6 × 2	5 × 5	9 × 1	2 × 4
3 × 7	7 × 0	0 × 9	3 × 6	7 × 5
5 × 6	3 × 2	4 × 2	7 × 4	3 × 3
1 × 9	2 × 7	0 × 6	1 × 3	4 × 5

MATH

factor   6 ———→ Find the **6**-row.
factor   × 8 ———→ Find the **8**-column.
product 4 8 ←——— The product is
                         named where
                         the 6-row and the
                         8-column meet.

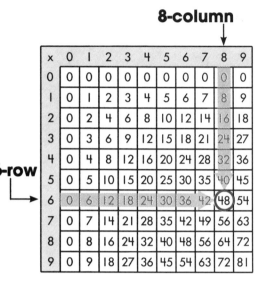

Directions: Multiply.

3		7		5		7
× 9		× 6		× 4		× 9
27						

| 8 | | 5 | | 4 | | 8 |
| ×   6 | | ×   0 | | ×   3 | | ×   5 |

| 4 | | 3 | | 5 | | 2 |
| ×   9 | | ×   0 | | ×   7 | | ×   9 |

Directions: Multiply.

5 × 1	4 × 6	8 × 2	6 × 8	4 × 0
0 × 9	3 × 1	6 × 4	9 × 2	3 × 4
6 × 3	5 × 6	3 × 8	3 × 6	7 × 6
9 × 9	8 × 4	5 × 3	2 × 6	8 × 8
9 × 3	7 × 4	8 × 0	7 × 7	9 × 8

Skill 24: Multiplying by Multiples of 10

	Multiply 0 ones by 4.	Multiply 7 tens by 4.
$\begin{array}{r} 70 \\ \times\ 4 \\ \hline \end{array}$	$\begin{array}{r} 70 \\ \times\ 4 \\ \hline 0 \end{array}$	$\begin{array}{r} 70 \\ \times\ 4 \\ \hline 280 \end{array}$

Directions: Multiply.

$\begin{array}{r} 30 \\ \times\ 3 \\ \hline 90 \end{array}$	$\begin{array}{r} 20 \\ \times\ 1 \\ \hline \end{array}$	$\begin{array}{r} 10 \\ \times\ 9 \\ \hline \end{array}$	$\begin{array}{r} 60 \\ \times\ 4 \\ \hline \end{array}$	$\begin{array}{r} 80 \\ \times\ 2 \\ \hline \end{array}$
$\begin{array}{r} 70 \\ \times\ 7 \\ \hline \end{array}$	$\begin{array}{r} 40 \\ \times\ 5 \\ \hline \end{array}$	$\begin{array}{r} 50 \\ \times\ 8 \\ \hline \end{array}$	$\begin{array}{r} 90 \\ \times\ 6 \\ \hline \end{array}$	$\begin{array}{r} 40 \\ \times\ 2 \\ \hline \end{array}$
$\begin{array}{r} 80 \\ \times\ 5 \\ \hline \end{array}$	$\begin{array}{r} 60 \\ \times\ 8 \\ \hline \end{array}$	$\begin{array}{r} 90 \\ \times\ 2 \\ \hline \end{array}$	$\begin{array}{r} 10 \\ \times\ 5 \\ \hline \end{array}$	$\begin{array}{r} 20 \\ \times\ 7 \\ \hline \end{array}$
$\begin{array}{r} 50 \\ \times\ 3 \\ \hline \end{array}$	$\begin{array}{r} 70 \\ \times\ 3 \\ \hline \end{array}$	$\begin{array}{r} 30 \\ \times\ 5 \\ \hline \end{array}$	$\begin{array}{r} 20 \\ \times\ 4 \\ \hline \end{array}$	$\begin{array}{r} 10 \\ \times\ 3 \\ \hline \end{array}$

Directions: Multiply.

90 × 4	70 × 9	60 × 2	50 × 5	20 × 5
50 × 3	10 × 3	10 × 4	30 × 4	50 × 2
30 × 5	10 × 4	30 × 6	20 × 2	70 × 3
40 × 3	40 × 4	80 × 2	40 × 6	20 × 7
50 × 6	50 × 5	40 × 8	90 × 0	70 × 5
40 × 9	30 × 2	10 × 8	60 × 5	80 × 8

MATH

Skill 25: Understanding Division

To divide means to make equal groups or to share equally. The answer to a division problem is called the **quotient**.

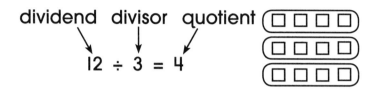

dividend   divisor   quotient

$$12 \div 3 = 4$$

Directions: Write each missing number.

$$\underline{6} \div \underline{2} = \underline{3}$$

$$\underline{} \div \underline{} = \underline{}$$

$$\underline{} \div \underline{} = \underline{}$$

$$\underline{} \div \underline{} = \underline{}$$

$$\underline{} \div \underline{} = \underline{}$$

$$\underline{} \div \underline{} = \underline{}$$

MATH

Skill 25: Understanding Division

Directions: Circle to show a fair share. Write the division sentence. Write how many each person gets.

Share with 3. _____

Each gets _____ .

Share with 6. _____

Each gets _____ .

Share with 8. _____

Each gets _____ .

Share with 2. _____

Each gets _____ .

Share with 2. _____

Each gets _____ .

Share with 3. _____

Each gets _____ .

MATH

26: Dividing Through 27 ÷ 3

$$\begin{array}{r} 5 \\ \times\ 3 \\ \hline 15 \end{array} \longrightarrow \begin{array}{r} 5 \\ 3\overline{)15} \end{array}$$

If 3 × 5 = 15, then 15 ÷ 3 = 5.

$$\begin{array}{r} 6 \\ \times\ 2 \\ \hline 12 \end{array} \longrightarrow \begin{array}{r} 6 \\ 2\overline{)12} \end{array}$$

If 2 × 6 = 12, then 12 ÷ 2 = 6.

Directions: Divide. Under each division problem, write the corresponding multiplication problem.

$$3\overline{)6}^{\,2}$$
3 × 2 = 6

$$2\overline{)14}$$

$$1\overline{)5}$$

$$2\overline{)4}$$

$$1\overline{)4}$$

$$3\overline{)27}$$

$$1\overline{)3}$$

$$2\overline{)18}$$

$$1\overline{)7}$$

Directions: Divide. Under each division problem, write the corresponding multiplication problem.

$3\overline{)12}$ $2\overline{)16}$ $1\overline{)5}$

$3\overline{)18}$ $2\overline{)10}$ $1\overline{)6}$

$1\overline{)8}$ $2\overline{)8}$ $1\overline{)2}$

$1\overline{)1}$ $3\overline{)24}$ $3\overline{)9}$

$1\overline{)9}$ $2\overline{)6}$ $2\overline{)2}$

$$\begin{array}{r} 5 \\ \times\ 4 \\ \hline 20 \end{array} \quad\longrightarrow\quad 4\overline{)20}\ {}^{5}$$

If 4 × 5 = 20, then 20 ÷ 4 = 5.

$$\begin{array}{r} 8 \\ \times\ 6 \\ \hline 48 \end{array} \quad\longrightarrow\quad 6\overline{)48}\ {}^{8}$$

If 6 × 8 = 48, then 48 ÷ 6 = 8.

Directions: Divide. Under each division problem, write the corresponding multiplication problem.

$6\overline{)54}\ {}^{9}$

6 × 9 = 54

$3\overline{)27}$

$6\overline{)48}$

$5\overline{)25}$

$4\overline{)36}$

$5\overline{)30}$

$4\overline{)24}$

$4\overline{)32}$

$4\overline{)16}$

Directions: Divide.

$6\overline{)36}$ $\qquad$ $4\overline{)28}$ $\qquad$ $5\overline{)35}$ $\qquad$ $6\overline{)24}$

$3\overline{)21}$ $\qquad$ $5\overline{)45}$ $\qquad$ $6\overline{)12}$ $\qquad$ $5\overline{)40}$

$3\overline{)24}$ $\qquad$ $6\overline{)18}$ $\qquad$ $3\overline{)12}$ $\qquad$ $2\overline{)16}$

$4\overline{)12}$ $\qquad$ $2\overline{)18}$ $\qquad$ $3\overline{)9}$ $\qquad$ $5\overline{)15}$

$6\overline{)42}$ $\qquad$ $3\overline{)18}$ $\qquad$ $6\overline{)6}$ $\qquad$ $3\overline{)27}$

MATH

28: Dividing Through 81 ÷ 9

$$\begin{array}{r} 6 \\ \times\ 9 \\ \hline 54 \end{array}$$ - - - - - - ▶ 6
- - - - ▶ $9\overline{)54}$

$$\begin{array}{r} 9 \\ \times\ 7 \\ \hline 63 \end{array}$$ - - - - - - ▶ 9
- - - - ▶ $7\overline{)63}$

If $9 \times 6 = 54$, then $54 \div 9 = 6$.

If $7 \times 9 = 63$, then $63 \div 7 = 9$.

Directions: Divide. Under each division problem, write the corresponding multiplication problem.

$7\overline{)7}$ with quotient 1

$7 \times 1 = 7$

$6\overline{)24}$

$8\overline{)56}$

$6\overline{)30}$

$8\overline{)64}$

$6\overline{)12}$

$7\overline{)35}$

$8\overline{)24}$

$7\overline{)28}$

100 Third Grade Skills

Skill 28: Dividing Through 81 ÷ 9

Directions: Divide.

$9\overline{)63}$ $9\overline{)81}$ $7\overline{)56}$ $5\overline{)35}$

$8\overline{)24}$ $9\overline{)18}$ $7\overline{)14}$ $7\overline{)21}$

$8\overline{)48}$ $9\overline{)45}$ $7\overline{)49}$ $8\overline{)16}$

$9\overline{)27}$ $9\overline{)9}$ $7\overline{)42}$ $9\overline{)27}$

$9\overline{)54}$ $8\overline{)8}$ $6\overline{)54}$ $8\overline{)40}$

MATH

Skill 29: Parts of a Whole

A fraction is a number for part of a whole.

$\frac{1}{4}$ ← numerator (part of the whole)
← denominator (parts in all)

 $\frac{1}{4}$ ← part shaded
← parts in all

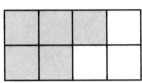 $\frac{5}{8}$ ← parts shaded
← parts in all

$\frac{1}{4}$ of the square is shaded. $\frac{5}{8}$ of the rectangle is shaded.

Directions: What fraction of each figure is shaded?

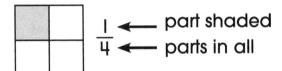

$\frac{1}{3}$ _____

_____

_____

_____

_____

_____

Skill 29: Parts of a Whole

Directions: What fraction of each figure is shaded?

_____

_____

_____

_____

_____

_____

MATH

A fraction is a number for part of a set.

$\dfrac{1}{2}$ ← numerator (part of the set)
← denominator (parts in all the set)

$\dfrac{1}{2}$ ← part shaded
← parts in all the set

$\dfrac{2}{3}$ ← parts shaded
← parts in all the set

Directions: What fraction of each set is shaded?

$\dfrac{4}{5}$

_____

_____

_____

_____

_____

MATH

30: Parts of a Set

Directions: What fraction of each set is shaded?

_____   _____   _____

Directions: Shade the number indicated by the fraction.

$\triangle \triangle \triangle \triangle$
$\triangle \triangle \triangle \triangle$

$\dfrac{4}{8}$

$\bigcirc \bigcirc$
$\bigcirc \bigcirc$

$\dfrac{3}{4}$

$\square \square \square \square \square$
$\square \square \square \square \square$

$\dfrac{3}{10}$

$\triangle \triangle \triangle$
$\triangle \triangle$

$\dfrac{1}{5}$

MATH

Skill 31: Comparing Fractions

When comparing fractions, look at the numerators and denominators.

If the **numerators** are the same, compare the denominators. The fraction with the smaller denominator is divided into fewer, larger pieces. So, it is the greater fraction.

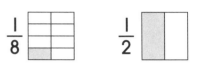

If the **denominators** are the same, compare the numerators. The fraction with the bigger numerator has more of the same-size pieces. So, it is the greater fraction.

Directions: Identify each fraction. Circle the greater fraction.

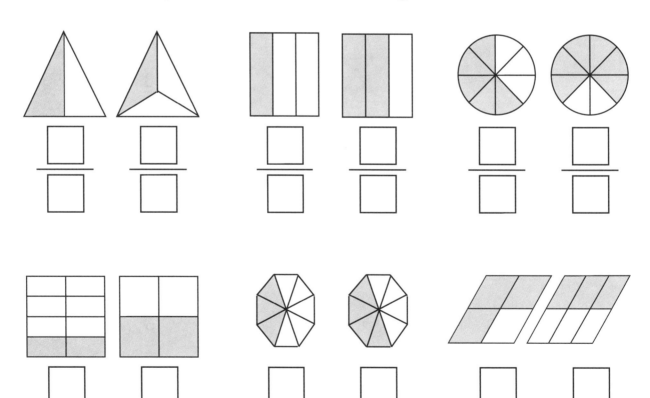

Directions: Compare using >, <, or =.

$\frac{5}{10} \bigcirc \frac{2}{10}$ $\frac{1}{3} \bigcirc \frac{2}{3}$ $\frac{5}{8} \bigcirc \frac{6}{8}$

$\frac{3}{10} \bigcirc \frac{8}{10}$ $\frac{1}{4} \bigcirc \frac{3}{4}$ $\frac{6}{7} \bigcirc \frac{3}{7}$

$\frac{4}{6} \bigcirc \frac{1}{6}$ $\frac{5}{9} \bigcirc \frac{4}{9}$ $\frac{6}{11} \bigcirc \frac{9}{11}$

$\frac{1}{5} \bigcirc \frac{3}{5}$ $\frac{3}{4} \bigcirc \frac{2}{4}$ $\frac{2}{3} \bigcirc \frac{1}{3}$

$\frac{1}{2} \bigcirc \frac{1}{4}$ $\frac{1}{3} \bigcirc \frac{2}{3}$ $\frac{3}{4} \bigcirc \frac{1}{4}$

MATH

32: Understanding Fractions on a Number Line

Fractions can be represented on a number line.

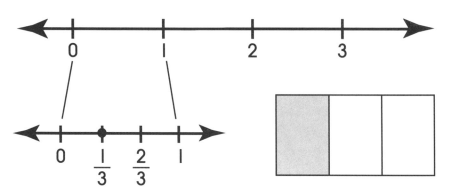

Both the number line and the rectangle represent the fraction $\frac{1}{3}$.

Directions: Use the number lines to answer the questions.

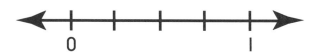

The number line is divided into _____ parts.

Label the number line with the correct fractions.

Each section of the number line represents what fraction? _____

Draw a dot to show the location of $\frac{2}{4}$.

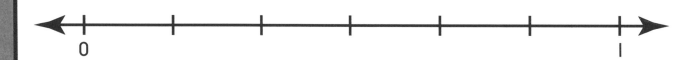

The number line is divided into _____ parts.

Label the number line with the correct fractions.

Each section of the number line represents what fraction? _____

Draw a dot to show the location of $\frac{5}{6}$.

MATH

32: Understanding Fractions on a Number Line

Directions: Use the number lines to answer the questions.

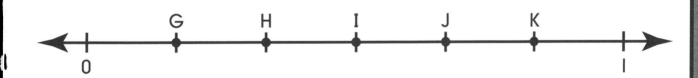

Label each number line with the correct fractions.

Which dot shows the location of $\frac{3}{6}$? _____

Which dot shows the location of $\frac{1}{3}$? _____

Which dot shows the location of $\frac{1}{6}$? _____

Which dot shows the location of $\frac{2}{4}$? _____

Draw a dot to represent each of the fractions below. Label them with the letter given.

L. $\frac{2}{2}$ M. $\frac{6}{6}$ N. $\frac{3}{3}$ O. $\frac{4}{4}$

MATH

Skill 33: Representing Fractions on a Number Line

To show a fraction on a number line, draw a number line with 0 and 1 as the endpoints.

Then, divide it into equal parts and label them.

Finally, draw a dot on the line to represent the fraction.

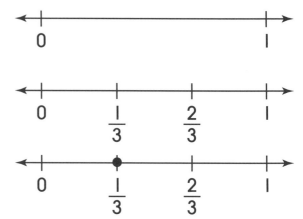

Directions: Show each fraction on the number line.

$\frac{2}{3}$

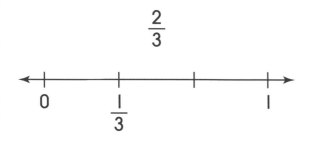

$\frac{3}{4}$

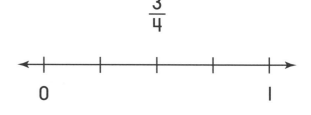

$\frac{1}{2}$

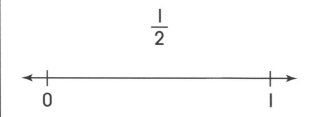

$\frac{5}{6}$

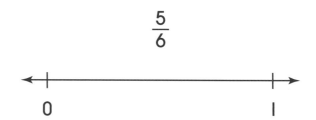

$\frac{1}{4}$

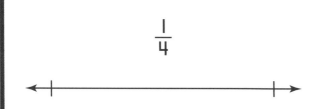

$\frac{7}{8}$

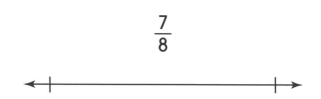

Skill 33: Representing Fractions on a Number Line

Directions: Show each fraction on the number line.

$$\frac{1}{4}$$

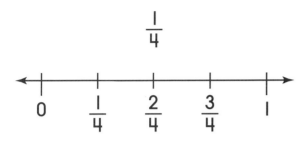

$$\frac{3}{6}$$

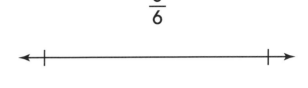

$$\frac{1}{3}$$

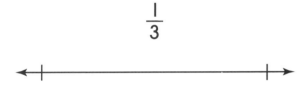

$$\frac{1}{6}$$

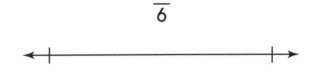

$$\frac{2}{4}$$

$$\frac{5}{8}$$

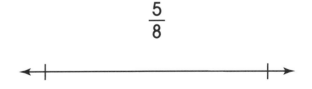

MATH

Skill 34: Whole Numbers as Fractions

= 1 $= \frac{4}{4} = 1$ $= \frac{2}{2} = 1$

Directions: Complete the fractions.

$= \frac{4}{4}$

= ____

= ____

= ____

= ____

= ____

= ____

= ____

100 Third Grade Skills

Skill 34: Whole Numbers as Fractions

Directions: Complete the fractions.

= ____

= ____

= ____

= ____

= ____

= ____

= ____

= ____

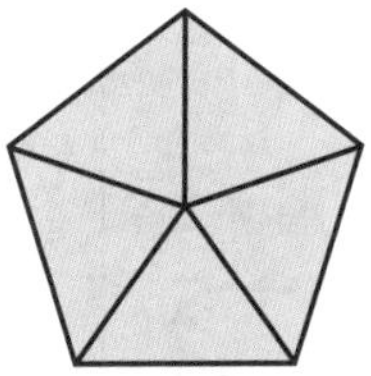

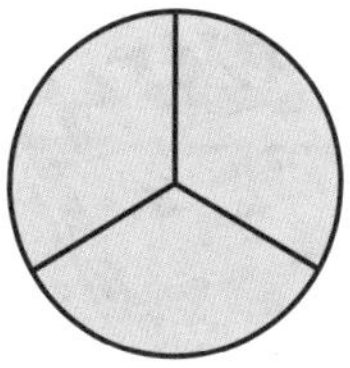

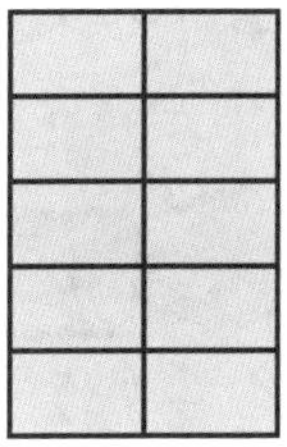

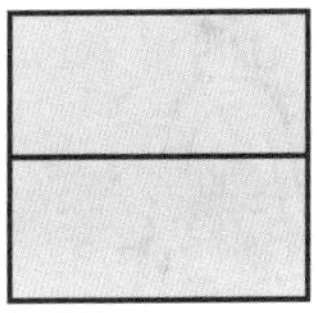

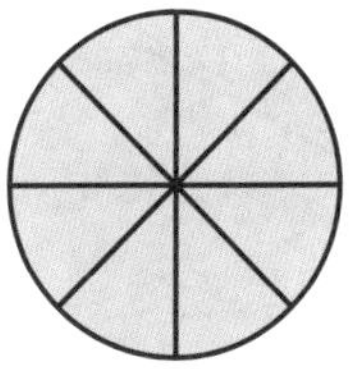

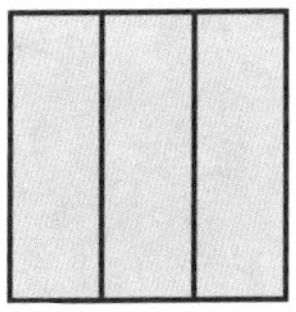

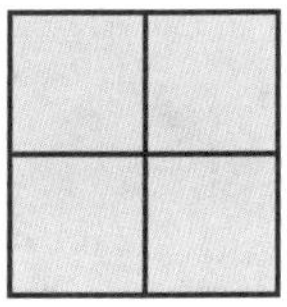

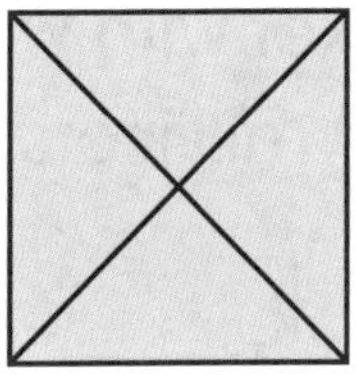

Metric units of mass
1,000 grams = 1 kilogram
1,000 g = 1 kg

1 kilogram (kg)

1 gram (g)

Metric units of volume
1,000 millimeters = 1 liter
1,000 mL = 1 L

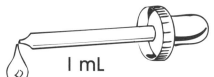

1 mL   1 L

Directions: Circle the correct unit to measure the following items.

g   kg   mL   L   g   kg   g   kg

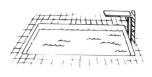   

mL   L   mL   L   g   kg

Directions: Solve.

Mrs. Murphy filled a bucket with water to mop the floor. Does her bucket probably hold 10 milliliters or 10 liters of water?

_____

A party hat has a mass of 30 grams. What is the mass of 8 party hats?

_____

Directions: Circle the best estimate.

g   kg

mL   L

g   kg

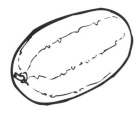

g   kg

mL   L

g   kg

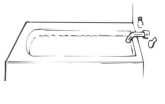

mL   L

Directions: Solve.

Jenna packed 15 kilograms of apples equally into 3 bags. How many kilograms of apples were in each bag?

_____

An adult weighs about 63 kilograms. An adult male moose weighs 396 kilograms. How much more does a moose weigh than a human?

_____

MATH

36: Picture Graphs

A **picture graph** uses symbols to represent data. The key tells you the value of each symbol on the picture graph.

Use the frequency table to complete the graph.

Students' Hair Color

Brown	⚇ ⚇ ⚇ ⚇ ⚇ ⚇ ⚇
Black	⚇ ⚇ ⚇ ⚇ ⚇
Blonde	⚇ ⚇ ⚇ ⚇ ⚇ ⚇
Red	⚇ ⚇

Frequency Table

Brown	⊞⊞ ⊞⊞ IIII
Black	⊞⊞ ⊞⊞
Blonde	⊞⊞ ⊞⊞ I
Red	III

Key: ⚇ = 2 students

How many students have red hair?

Each stick figure represents two students.

Count by twos when counting the stick figures in the row labeled "red." Add 1 to the sum for the half stick figure.

___3___ students have red hair.

Directions: Complete the picture graph. Answer the question.

Flowers In My Garden

Frequency Table

Daisies	⊞⊞ III
Roses	⊞⊞
Sunflowers	II

Key: 🏵 = 2 flowers

How many total flowers are in the garden? _____

Directions: Use the information in the charts to complete the graphs.

Growth (in cm)	
A	
B	
C	
D	
E	

Key: ✿ = 10 cm

Plant Food	Growth (in cm)
A	20
B	30
C	50
D	10
E	40

Flowers We Planted	
Rm 102	
Rm 103	
Rm 104	
Rm 105	

Key: ✿ = 5 flowers

Classroom	Flowers Planted
Room 102	35
Room 103	25
Room 104	20
Room 105	25

Students' Favorite Sport

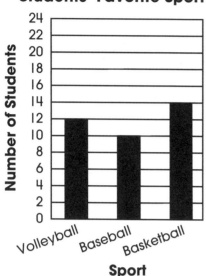

A **bar graph** uses rectangular bars to represent data.

Use the frequency table to complete the graph.

Frequency Table

Volleyball	12
Baseball	10
Basketball	14

How many students chose baseball as their favorite sport?

Find the bar labeled baseball.

Follow the top of the bar to the scale at the left.

This value represents the number of students whose favorite sport is baseball.

___10___ students chose baseball as their favorite sport.

Directions: Complete the bar graph. Answer the question.

Candle Sale Totals

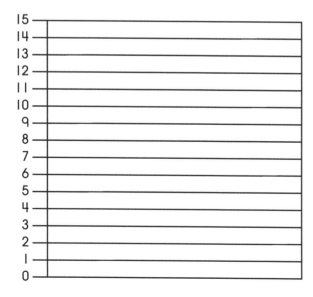

Frequency Table

Abbie	10
Brady	15
Denise	6

How many more candles did Brady sell than Denise?

_____

MATH

Skill 37: Bar Graphs

Directions: Use the information in the charts to complete the graphs. Then, use the graphs to answer the questions.

How many more students voted for sea lions than birds? _____

How many more students voted for snakes than elephants? _____

Animal	Votes
elephant	12
sea lion	15
bird	6
snake	18

Food Items	Number Sold
hot dogs	30
hamburgers	50
chips	50
fries	30
fruit bowls	60
ice cream	40

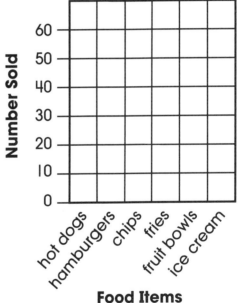

Concession Stand Sales

How many fruit bowls and ice cream treats were sold altogether?

_____

Which two items sold the least? _____

Which item was sold the most? _____

How many more chips were sold than fries? _____

Skill 38: Line Plots

A **line plot** is a type of graph that shows information on a number line.

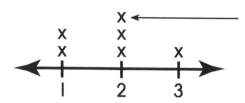

Line plots are useful for showing frequency, or the number of times something is repeated.

Directions: Use a ruler to measure 8 things to the nearest $\frac{1}{2}$ inch. Record your data in the table.

Item	Length	Item	Length

Directions: Use the data from the table to make a line plot. Look at the data and decide what numbers you will need to include. Mark each number on the line plot and label it. Do not leave out numbers in between, even if they have no data. Mark each data point with an X.

Directions: Use a ruler to measure 10 things to the nearest $\frac{1}{2}$ inch. Record your data in the table.

Item	Length	Item	Length

Directions: Use the data from the table to make a line plot. Remember to look at your data to see what numbers you need to represent. Then, divide and label the line. Mark each data point with an X.

Area is the number of square units it takes to cover the surface of a figure.

To find area, count the number of squares it takes to cover the shape. The squares must touch along the edges with no overlap and no gaps.

Area is measured in *square units*, such as *square inches* or *square centimeters*. If the unit is not known, you can use *square units* as shown in the example.

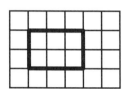

Area (A) = 6 square units

Directions: Find the area of each figure.

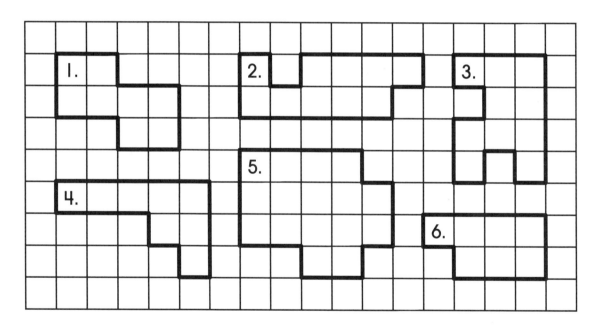

1. A = _____ sq. units

2. A = _____ sq. units

3. A = _____ sq. units

4. A = _____ sq. units

5. A = _____ sq. units

6. A = _____ sq. units

Skill 39: Finding Area With Unit Squares

Directions: Find the area of each figure.

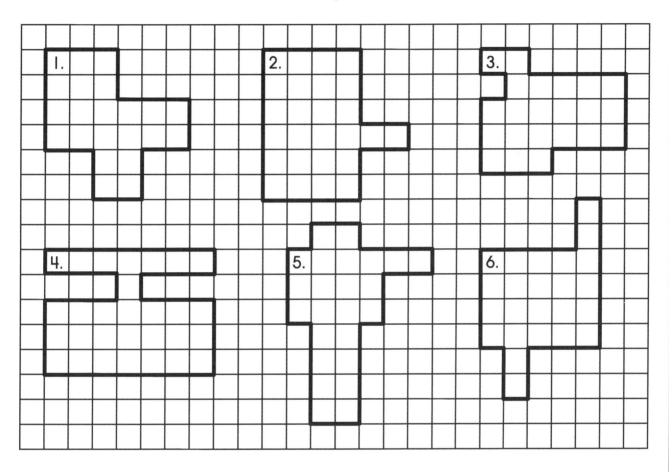

1. A = _____ sq. units

2. A = _____ sq. units

3. A = _____ sq. units

4. A = _____ sq. units

5. A = _____ sq. units

6. A = _____ sq. units

MATH

40: Measuring Area

To find the area of a square or rectangle, multiply length by width.

10 ft. (length)

2 ft. (width)

10 ft. × 2 ft. = 20 sq. ft.

The product is written as 20 square feet.

Draw the square units.

5 cm

3 cm

A = _____15_____ sq. cm

Multiply to check your answer.

_5_ × _3_ = _15_

A = _____15_____ sq. cm

Directions: Find the area of each shape.

15 in.

5 in.

_____75_____ sq. in.

8 ft.

7 ft.

_____ sq. ft.

7 yd.

25 yd.

_____ sq. yd.

5 in.

8 in.

_____ sq. in.

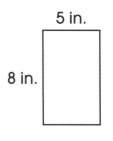

Directions: Draw the square units. Then, multiply to check your answer.

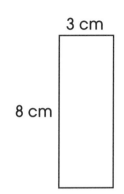

3 cm

8 cm

_____ × _____ = _____

A = _____ sq. cm

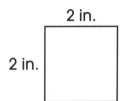

2 in.

2 in.

_____ × _____ = _____

A = _____ sq. in.

4 cm

1 cm

_____ × _____ = _____

A = _____ sq. cm

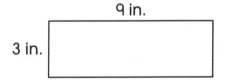

9 in.

3 in.

_____ × _____ = _____

A = _____ sq. in.

5 cm

3 cm

_____ × _____ = _____

A = _____ sq. cm

4 in

5 in

_____ × _____ = _____

A = _____ sq. in.

MATH

Divide the figure into recognizable shapes.

Find the area of each individual shape.

Then, add the areas together to find the total area of the shape.

Directions: Find the area of each figure.

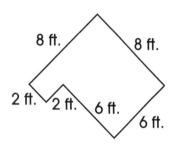

A = _____ 52 sq. ft. _____

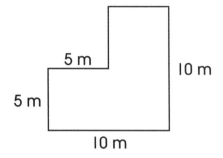

A = _____

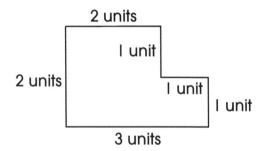

A = _____

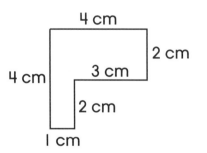

A = _____

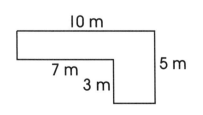

A = _____

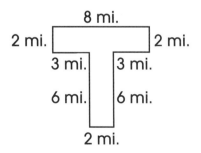

A = _____

Directions: Find the area of each figure.

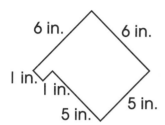

A = _____

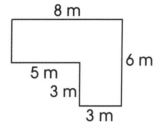

A = _____

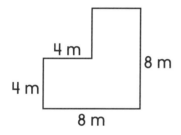

A = _____

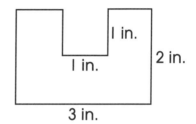

A = _____

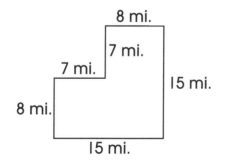

A = _____

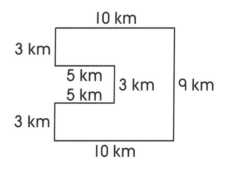

A = _____

Skill 42: Measuring Perimeter

Perimeter is the total distance around a given figure. To find the perimeter, add the lengths of the sides together.

Example: P = perimeter

P = 4 cm + 8 cm + 4 cm + 8 cm

P = 24 cm

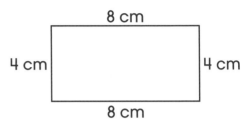

Directions: Find the perimeter of each figure.

4 yd.

2 yd.

P = _____

6 ft.

3 ft.

P = _____

19 ft.

5 ft.

P = _____

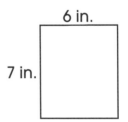

6 in.

7 in.

P = _____

8 in.

8 in.

P = _____

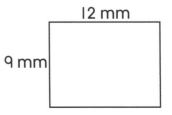

12 mm

9 mm

P = _____

Directions: Find the perimeter of each figure.

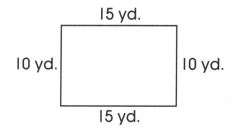

P = 15 + 10 + 15 + 10

P = _____

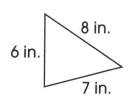

P = _____

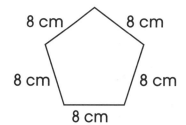

P = _____

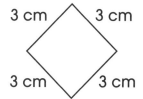

P = _____

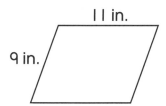

P = _____

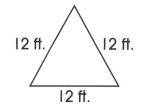

P = _____

Mrs. Young's tennis court is a rectangle that is 30 feet wide by 70 feet long. What is the perimeter?

P = _____

A square tile has sides that are 15 inches each. What is the perimeter?

P = _____

A hexagon has sides that are 5 millimeters each. What is the perimeter?

P = _____

Skill 43: Telling Time

 6:15 is read "six fifteen" and means "15 minutes after 6."

 12:50 is read "twelve fifty" and means "50 minutes after 12" or "10 minutes to 1."

 5:45 is read "five forty-five" and means "45 minutes after 5" or "15 minutes to 6."

6:41

The closest hour on an analog clock is determined by the hour hand (the short hand).

The closest half hour, quarter hour, and minute are determined by the minute hand (the long hand).

A half hour is at 30 minutes or 1 hour.

A quarter hour is at 15, 30, 45 minutes, or 1 hour.

What time is it to the nearest hour? __7:00__, half hour? __6:30__, quarter hour? __6:45__, minute? __6:41__

Directions: Complete the following.

6:15 means __15__ minutes after __6__. | 12:50 means ___ minutes to ___.

8:50 means ___ minutes after ___. | 6:50 means ___ minutes to ___.

3:45 means ___ minutes after ___. | 7:45 means ___ minutes to ___.

2:30 means ___ minutes after ___. | 1:30 means ___ minutes to ___.

MATH

Skill 43: Telling Time

Directions: Write the time to the nearest hour, half hour, quarter hour, or minute as indicated.

hour	half hour	quarter hour	minute
___ : ___	___ : ___	___ : ___	___ : ___

Directions: Draw the hands on the analog clock to express the time presented on the digital clock.

Directions: For each analog clock face, write the numerals that name the time.

___ : ___   ___ : ___   ___ : ___   ___ : ___

Jesse gets up at 6:30 a.m. She leaves the house at 8:20 a.m. How much time passed between when she got up and left the house?

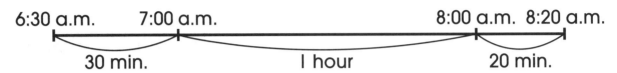

| 6:30 a.m. | 7:00 a.m. | | 8:00 a.m. | 8:20 a.m. |

| 30 min. | 1 hour | 20 min. |

First, find out how much time until the next hour.

Second, find out how much time passed since the previous hour.

Then, find out how much time passed between the next hour and the previous hour.

Last, add up the minutes and hours to find out the total time that has passed.

_____1 hour, 50 minutes_____

Directions: Solve.

Sam went to the bookstore at 6:45 p.m. He left the bookstore at 10:10 p.m. How long was Sam at the bookstore?

_____

6:45 p.m.   10:10 p.m.

Darcy leaves for work at 8:45 a.m. She leaves work to go home at 5:15 p.m. How much time does Darcy spend at work?

_____

8:45 a.m.   5:15 p.m.

MATH

Directions: Solve. Show the elapsed time on the number line.

Casey left for work at 2:15 p.m. He ate dinner at 7:15 p.m. How much time passed between the time Casey left work and ate dinner?

_____

2:15 p.m.   7:15 p.m.

Sharon takes her puppy to the park at 8:40 a.m. She goes to the lake, then to a friend's house, and gets home at 12:10 p.m. How much time was Sharon out of the house?

_____

8:40 a.m.   12:10 p.m.

Jose goes to school at 7:50 a.m. The last bell rings at 2:05 p.m. How much time is Jose at school?

_____

7:50 a.m.   2:05 p.m.

MATH

A **plane figure** is a flat surface.

circle   triangle   square   rectangle

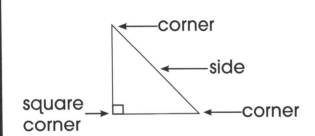

Each side of a triangle, square, and rectangle is a **line segment**.

The point where two line segments meet is a **corner** or a **square corner**.

A square corner is a right angle. A right angle has a measure of 90°.

Directions: Draw the following plane figures.

triangle   rectangle

square   circle

Skill 45: Plane Figures

Directions: Complete the following.

	number of sides	number of square corners	number of other corners
○	0	_____	_____
▭	_____	_____	_____
◿	_____	I	_____
□	_____	_____	_____
△	_____	0	_____

MATH

Skill 46: Solid Figures

A **solid figure** is a three-dimensional object. Solid figures may be hollow or solid.

 cube

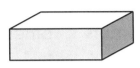 rectangular prism

 square pyramid

 sphere

 cylinder

 cone

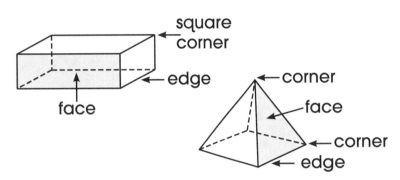

A **face** is the shape formed by the edges of a solid figure.

An **edge** is where 2 faces meet.

A **vertex** or **corner** is the point where 2 or more edges come together.

Directions: Complete the table.

Solid Figure	Number of Square Faces	Number of Rectangle Faces	Number of Triangle Faces
cube			0
rectangular prism			
square pyramid	1		

MATH

Skill 46: Solid Figures

Directions: Answer the questions.

How many edges does a sphere have? _____ edges

How many edges does a square pyramid have? _____ edges

How many edges does a cube have? _____ edges

How many edges does a rectangular prism have? _____ edges

How many corners does a square pyramid have? _____ corners

How many corners does a rectangular prism have? _____ corners

Directions: Give a physical example of each of the following plane figures.

cube	rectangular prism
sugar cube	_____
square pyramid	sphere
_____	_____
cylinder	cone
_____	_____

MATH

Quadrilaterals are four-sided shapes. To be a quadrilateral, all four sides must be connected.

Parallelograms are quadrilaterals with two sets of parallel sides.

Rectangles are parallelograms with four right angles.

Rhombuses are parallelograms with four sides of equal length.

Squares are rectangles with four equal sides. They are also rhombuses with four right angles.

Directions: Circle the shapes named.

Circle the quadrilaterals.

Circle the parallelograms.

Circle the rectangles.

Skill 47: Classifying Quadrilaterals

Directions: Circle the shapes named. Then, answer the question.

Circle the rhombuses.

Circle the squares.

Which of the shapes defined above fits into all five categories?

_____

Directions: Name each four-sided figure.

_____ _____ _____ _____

Directions: How many sides or edges are there on these figures?

_____ _____ _____ _____

: Dividing Shapes

Halves = 2 equal pieces

Thirds = 3 equal pieces

Fourths = 4 equal pieces

Fifths = 5 equal pieces

Divide this shape into thirds.

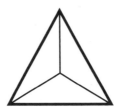

Label each third.

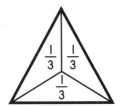

Directions: Divide each shape into the given amount of equal parts. Then, label each piece with the appropriate fraction.

halves

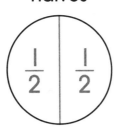

thirds

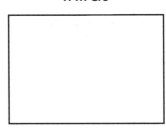

thirds

halves

MATH

Skill 48: Dividing Shapes

Directions: Divide each shape into the given amount of equal parts. Then, label each piece with the appropriate fraction.

fourths

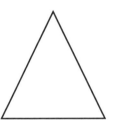

fifths

halves

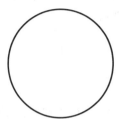

fourths

fifths

thirds

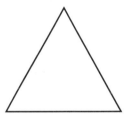

halves

fourths

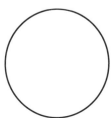

SKILL 49: Number Patterns

A number pattern can be developed by addition or subtraction.

Complete this pattern by subtraction.

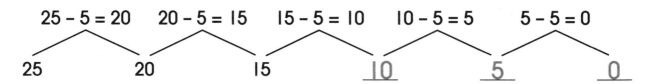

$$25 - 5 = 20 \quad 20 - 5 = 15 \quad 15 - 5 = 10 \quad 10 - 5 = 5 \quad 5 - 5 = 0$$

25 20 15 <u>10</u> <u>5</u> <u>0</u>

Directions: Complete the pattern by using addition or subtraction.

| 2 | 4 | 6 | _____ | _____ | _____ |

| 1 | 3 | 5 | _____ | _____ | _____ |

| 20 | 18 | 16 | _____ | _____ | _____ |

| 21 | 15 | 10 | _____ | _____ | _____ |

| 18 | 15 | 12 | _____ | _____ | _____ |

| 6 | 13 | 21 | _____ | _____ | _____ |

| 30 | 29 | 26 | 21 | _____ | _____ |

Directions: Complete the pattern by using addition or subtraction.

13	12	11	_____	_____	_____
5	10	15	_____	_____	_____
3	6	9	_____	_____	_____
10	20	40	_____	_____	_____
16	13	10	_____	_____	_____
10	9	8	_____	_____	_____
24	20	16	_____	_____	_____
2	9	16	_____	_____	_____
250	245	235	220	_____	_____

MATH

A **number sentence** is an equation with numbers.

Identity Property	**Commutative Property**
for addition: $0 + 3 = 3$	for addition: $3 + 2 = 2 + 3$
for multiplication: $1 \times 3 = 3$	for multiplication: $4 \times 2 = 2 \times 4$

A number sentence can change its look but not change its value.

$3 + 5 = 8$ or $3 + 5 = 4 + 4$ $\qquad$ $3 \times 8 = 24$ or $3 \times 8 = 6 \times 4$

Associative Property	**Distributive Property**
$(2 \times 3) \times 4 = c$	$6 + 5 = 11$
$2 \times 3 = 6$	$11 \times 8 = (6 \times 8) + (5 \times 8)$
$6 \times 4 = 24$	$48 + 40 = 88$
$c = 24$	$11 \times 8 = 88$

Directions: Complete each number sentence.

$0 + 4 = \boxed{4}$ $\qquad$ $0 + 6 = \boxed{}$ $\qquad$ $\boxed{} + 2 = 2$

$1 \times 2 = \boxed{}$ $\qquad$ $1 \times 5 = \boxed{}$ $\qquad$ $\boxed{} \times 4 = 4$

$7 + 2 = \boxed{} + 7$ $\qquad$ $3 + 4 = \boxed{} + 3$ $\qquad$ $1 + 2 = 2 + \boxed{}$

Directions: Complete the following.

$2 + 7 = 9$ or $\qquad$ $5 + 7 = 12$ or $\qquad$ $4 + 3 = 7$ or

$2 + 7 = 5 + \boxed{4}$ $\qquad$ $5 + 7 = 6 + \boxed{}$ $\qquad$ $4 + 3 = 5 + \boxed{}$

$6 + 4 = 10$ or $\qquad$ $6 + 7 = 13$ or $\qquad$ $5 + 3 = 8$ or

$6 + 4 = 5 + \boxed{}$ $\qquad$ $6 + 7 = 8 + \boxed{}$ $\qquad$ $5 + 3 = 6 + \boxed{}$

Directions: Solve using the associative property.

$3 \times 5 \times 2 = d$

_____ × _____ = _____

_____ × _____ = _____

$d =$ _____

$2 \times 9 \times 1 = h$

_____ × _____ = _____

_____ × _____ = _____

$h =$ _____

$4 \times 6 \times 2 = e$

_____ × _____ = _____

_____ × _____ = _____

$e =$ _____

$7 \times 4 \times 2 = g$

_____ × _____ = _____

_____ × _____ = _____

$g =$ _____

Directions: Solve using the distributive property.

$12 \times 4 = (6 \times 4) + ($ _____ $\times 4)$

_____ + _____

$12 \times 4 =$ _____

$14 \times 3 = (8 \times 3) + ($ _____ $\times 3)$

_____ + _____

$14 \times 3 =$ _____

$19 \times 2 = (9 \times 2) + ($ _____ $\times 2)$

_____ + _____

$19 \times 2 =$ _____

$16 \times 5 = (7 \times 5) + ($ _____ $\times 5)$

_____ + _____

$16 \times 5 =$ _____

MATH

50
LANGUAGE
ARTS
SKILLS

A **common noun** names any person, place, or thing, rather than a specific person, place, or thing.

person    • magician
    • brother
    • girl

place    • tree house
    • park
    • closet

thing    • soap
    • pail
    • shoe

Directions: Name these nouns.

   person _____

   place _____

    thing _____

100 Third Grade Skills

Skill 51: Common Nouns

Directions: Read the sentences below and write the common noun that you find in each sentence. The first one is done for you.

1. _____socks_____ My socks do not match.

2. _____ The bird could not fly.

3. _____ Ben likes to eat jelly beans.

4. _____ I am going to meet my mother.

5. _____ We will go swimming in the lake tomorrow.

6. _____ I hope the flowers will grow quickly.

7. _____ We colored eggs together.

8. _____ It is easy to ride a bicycle.

9. _____ Please hand me my coat.

LANGUAGE ARTS

Skill 52: Proper Nouns

A **proper noun** names a specific person, place, or thing. A proper noun begins with a capital letter.

Directions: Read the sentences below and circle the proper nouns found in each sentence. The first one is done for you.

1. (Aunt Frances) gave me a puppy for my birthday.

2. We lived on Jackson Street before we moved to our new house.

3. Angela's birthday party is tomorrow night.

4. We drove through Cheyenne, Wyoming, on our way home.

5. Dr. Charles always gives me a treat for not crying.

6. George Washington was our first president.

7. Our class took a field trip to the Johnson Flower Farm.

8. Uncle Jack lives in New York City.

Directions: Write about you! Write a proper noun for each category below. Capitalize the first letter of each proper noun.

1. Your first name: _____

2. Your last name: _____

3. Your street: _____

4. Your city: _____

5. Your state: _____

6. Your country: _____

7. Your school: _____

8. Your best friend: _____

Skill 53: Abstract Nouns

Abstract nouns are nouns that you can't experience with your five senses. They are feelings, concepts, and ideas. Some examples are **friendship**, **childhood**, **bravery**, **hope**, and **pride**.

Directions: Underline the abstract noun in each sentence below.

1. Maya's honesty is one of the reasons we are best friends.

2. Her eyes were full of hope as she opened her report card.

3. We would like to see justice served.

4. I love the delight on my sister's face on her birthday.

5. Your kindness will not be forgotten.

6. Benji felt great pride when his team won the championship.

7. What are your parents' best stories about their childhood?

8. It is important to me that you always tell the truth.

Skill 53: Abstract Nouns

Directions: Fill in each blank below with an abstract noun from the box.

wisdom	joy	knowledge
courage	freedom	love

1. You can see the _____ this father has for his son.

2. It took great _____ to rebuild after the hurricane.

3. Uncle Zane's _____ of birds amazes me.

4. The room was filled with _____ when Will found his lost puppy.

5. It would be great to have the _____ to travel the world.

6. Grandpa has the _____ that comes with a long life.

Skill 54: Plural Nouns

A noun that names one thing, like **house**, is **singular**. A noun that names more than one thing, like **houses**, is **plural**.

To make most words plural, add **s**.

Example: one book — two books   one tree — four trees

To make words that end in **s**, **ss**, **x**, **sh**, and **ch** plural, add **es**.

Example: one fox — two foxes   one bush — three bushes

Directions: Add **s** or **es** to make each word plural.

1. pencil _____

2. peach _____

3. class _____

4. ax _____

5. bush _____

6. crash _____

To make a word that ends in **y** plural, change the **y** to **i** and add **es**.

Example: pony — ponies

Directions: Write the plural form of each noun.

1. baby _____

2. bunny _____

3. cherry _____

4. kitty _____

5. sky _____

6. candy _____

Skill 54: Plural Nouns

To make **plural nouns**:

Add **s** to most singular nouns ending in a vowel and the letter **o**.

Example: rodeo — rodeos

Add **es** to most singular nouns ending in a consonant and the letter **o**.

Example: tomato — tomatoes

Change the **f** to **v** and add **es** to singular nouns ending in **f**.

Example: leaf — leaves

Directions: Circle the correct plural form of each noun.

1. avocado	avocados	avocatos	avocatose
2. wolf	wolfs	wolves	wolvs
3. mosquito	mosquitoes	mosquitoz	mosquitos
4. halo	halos	haloes	haloz
5. knife	knives	knifs	knifes
6. zero	zeroes	zeros	zeroz
7. elf	elfs	elves	elfz
8. volcano	volcanoes	volcanos	volcanoese
9. shelf	shelfs	shelvs	shelves
10. hoof	hooves	hoofs	hoofes

Skill 55: Irregular Plural Nouns

Some words in the English language do not follow plural rules. These words may not change at all from singular to plural, or they may completely change spellings.

No Change Examples:

Singular	Plural
deer	deer
pants	pants
scissors	scissors
moose	moose
sheep	sheep

Complete Change Examples:

Singular	Plural
goose	geese
ox	oxen
man	men
child	children
leaf	leaves

Directions: Write the singular or plural form of each word. Use a dictionary to help you.

	Singular	Plural		Singular	Plural
1.	moose	_____	2.	leaf	_____
3.	woman	_____	4.	_____	sheep
5.	_____	deer	6.	scissors	_____
7.	_____	children	8.	tooth	_____
9.	_____	hooves	10.	wharf	_____

Directions: Write four sentences of your own using two singular and two plural words from above.

_____

_____

_____

_____

LANGUAGE ARTS

Skill 55: Irregular Plural Nouns

Directions: Match each phrase below to the correct plural form. Write the letter on the line.

1. _____ one bison   **a.** fifty bisons   **b.** fifty bison

2. _____ one die   **a.** six dice   **b.** six dies

3. _____ one offspring   **a.** many offspring   **b.** many offsprings

4. _____ the trout   **a.** hundreds of trout   **b.** hundreds of trouts

5. _____ one species   **a.** eight species   **b.** eight specieses

6. _____ the goose   **a.** four gooses   **b.** four geese

7. _____ one series   **a.** three serieses   **b.** three series

8. _____ a child   **a.** most childs   **b.** most children

Skill 56: Singular Possessive Nouns

To make a singular noun show **possession**, or ownership, add an apostrophe (') and the letter **s**.

Example: Deandre — **Deandre's** hiking shoes are muddy.

tree — The **tree's** limbs are heavy with snow.

Directions: Change each noun to its possessive form.

1. snake _____

2. lizard _____

3. bottle _____

4. flower _____

5. bird _____

6. pirate _____

Directions: Write a sentence using the possessive form of each word.

1. Bailey _____

_____

2. car _____

_____

3. bug _____

_____

4. flower _____

_____

5. bed _____

_____

LANGUAGE ARTS

Skill 56: Singular Possessive Nouns

Directions: Circle the correct possessive noun in each sentence and write it in the blank. The first one is done for you.

1. One _____girl's_____ dad is a doctor.
   (girl's)   girls'

2. The _____ tail is long.
   cat's   cats'

3. One _____ soccer ball is new.
   boy's   boys'

4. A _____ apron is white.
   waitresses'   waitress's

5. My _____ apple pie is the best!
   grandma's   grandmas'

6. The _____ hair is pretty.
   child's   childs'

7. This _____ collar is green.
   dog's   dogs'

8. The _____ tail is short.
   cow's   cows'

LANGUAGE ARTS

Skill 57: Plural Possessive Nouns

To make a plural noun ending in **s** show **possession** or ownership, add an apostrophe (') after the letter **s**.

Example: boys — The **boys'** mother took them to the skate park.

If the plural noun does not end in **s**, add an apostrophe (') and the letter **s**.

Example: men — The **men's** fitting room is on the left.

Directions: Change each plural noun to its possessive form.

1. cups _____

2. children _____

3. hamburgers _____

4. parents _____

5. french fries _____

6. milkshakes _____

7. workers _____

8. sundaes _____

9. straws _____

10. fish _____

LANGUAGE ARTS

Skill 57: Plural Possessive Nouns

Directions: Write a sentence using the possessive form of each plural noun.

1. girls _____

_____

2. women _____

_____

3. shirts _____

_____

4. cookies _____

_____

5. brothers _____

_____

6. igloos _____

_____

7. explorers _____

_____

8. bears _____

_____

9. peanuts _____

_____

LANGUAGE ARTS

Skill 58: Pronouns

A **pronoun** is a word that takes the place of a noun.

Example: he, she, it, they, him, them, her, him

Directions: Read each sentence. Write the pronoun that takes the place of each noun. The first one is done for you.

1. The **monkey** dropped the banana. _____ It

2. **Dad** washed the car last night. _____

3. **Dawn and Greg** took a walk in the park. _____

4. **Jessica** spent the night at her friend's house. _____

5. The basketball **players** lost their game. _____

6. **Lionel Messi** is a great soccer player. _____

7. The **parrot** can say five different words. _____

8. **Heather** wrote a report in class today. _____

9. They planned a party for **Naomi**. _____

10. Everyone in the class was happy for **Brad**. _____

LANGUAGE ARTS

Skill 58: Pronouns

Use the pronouns **I** and **we** when talking about the person or people doing the action.

Example: I can skate.
      We can skate.

Use the pronouns **me** and **us** when talking about the person or people receiving the action.

Example: They gave **me** the skates.
      They gave **us** the skates.

Directions: Circle the correct pronoun and write it in the blank. The first one is done for you.

1. _____We_____ are going to the show together.   **We**   **Us**

2. _____ am finished with my history project.   **I**   **Me**

3. Andrew passed the salt to _____ .   **me**   **I**

4. They ate lunch with _____ yesterday.   **we**   **us**

5. _____ had a pool party in our backyard.   **Us**   **We**

6. They told _____ the good news.   **us**   **we**

7. Jake and _____ went to the movies.   **me**   **I**

8. She is taking _____ with her to the concert.   **I**   **me**

Skill 59: Subject and Object Pronouns

A **subject pronoun** takes the place of a noun in the subject of a sentence.

An **object pronoun** takes the place of a noun that follows a verb or a word such as **to**, **from**, **of**, **at**, **with**, or **by**.

Subject Pronouns
I   you   he   she   it   we   they

Object Pronouns
me   you   him   her   it   us   you   them

Directions: Replace each underlined word or phrase with a subject or object pronoun. Rewrite each sentence.

1. <u>The third-grade class</u> went on a class trip to the aquarium.

   _____

2. <u>The aquarium</u> was filled with interesting sea life.

   _____

3. Janice shrieked when <u>Janice</u> saw the shark tank.

   _____

4. "<u>The sharks</u> have really sharp teeth," Janice said.

   _____

5. David reassured her, "<u>The sharks</u> can't hurt, Janice."

   _____

6. <u>Our class</u> believed David because <u>David</u> is the tour guide.

   _____

LANGUAGE ARTS

Skill 59: Subject and Object Pronouns

Directions: Read the sentences below. Cross out the incorrect pronouns. Then, write the correct pronouns above them.

1. The students in Ms. Curry's class are going on a field trip. Them are going to the museum.

2. Ms. Curry told we that the museum is her favorite field trip.

3. The bus will leave at 8:30 in the morning. She will be parked in the school's west lot.

4. Casey and Allison will sit together. Them are best friends.

5. Ibrahim or Peter might sit with I.

6. The Goose Creek museum is not far away. It did not take we long to drive to him.

7. Michael forgot to bring his lunch. Ms. Curry gave he half of her sandwich and an apple.

8. Me loved seeing all the fossils.

Skill 60: Verbs

A **verb** is the action word in a sentence. It is the word that tells what something does or that something exists.

Example: run, jump, skip

Directions: Draw a box around the verb in each sentence below.

1. Spiders spin webs of silk.

2. A spider waits in the center of the web for its meals.

3. A spider sinks its sharp fangs into insects.

4. Spiders eat many insects.

5. Spiders make their nests with silk.

6. Female spiders wrap silk around their eggs to protect them.

Directions: Choose the correct verb from the Word Bank to finish each sentence.

Word Bank		
hides	eats	grabs

1. A crab spider _____ deep inside a flower where it cannot be seen.

2. The crab spider _____ insects when they land on the flower.

3. The wolf spider is good because it _____ wasps.

LANGUAGE ARTS

Skill 60: Verbs

Directions: Write an action word from the Word Bank in each blank.

Word Bank			
dances	eats	rides	shoots

1. Brady _____ his new, red bike.

2. The girl _____ on the stage.

3. Coby _____ the arrow at the target.

4. Judy _____ pumpkin pie.

Directions: Write three sentences using verbs from the Word Bank.

Word Bank				
creates	hammers	builds	mows	scrubs

1. _____

_____

2. _____

_____

3. _____

_____

LANGUAGE ARTS

Skill 61: Linking Verbs

A **linking verb** connects the noun to a descriptive word. A linking verb is often a form of the verb **be**.

Directions: The linking verb is underlined in each sentence. Circle the two words that the linking verb connects.

Example: The (cat) is (fat.)

1. My favorite food <u>is</u> lasagna.

2. The car <u>was</u> blue.

3. I <u>am</u> tired.

4. Books <u>are</u> fun!

5. The garden <u>is</u> beautiful.

6. The pear <u>was</u> juicy.

7. The garage <u>is</u> large.

8. Rabbits <u>are</u> furry.

Directions: Write the correct linking verb (**am**, **is**, or **are**) to complete each sentence.

1. We _____ going to the pool today.

2. The day _____ perfect for soccer.

3. The students _____ happy.

4. She _____ the one who organized the party.

5. He _____ a good student.

6. I _____ tired from hiking all day.

7. They _____ going to the movies after school.

8. Mr. Johnson _____ the teacher.

9. I _____ excited about our trip!

10. You _____ my best friend.

LANGUAGE ARTS

Skill 62: The Verb Be

Most verbs name an action. The verb **be** is different. It tells about someone or something. **Am**, **is**, and **are** are forms of the verb **be**.

Use **is** with one person, place, or thing.

Example: Mrs. Jones **is** my principal.

Use **are** with more than one person, place, or thing or with the word **you**.

Example: We **are** studying presidents.   You **are** excited.

Use **am** with the word **I**.

Example: I **am** sad today.

Directions: Fill in each blank with the correct form of the verb **be** (**is**, **am**, or **are**).

1. My dog _____ brown.

2. My favorite color _____ green.

3. We _____ baking a cake today.

4. I _____ going to the movies on Saturday.

5. My friends _____ going with me.

6. What _____ your cell phone number?

LANGUAGE ARTS

Directions: Fill in each blank with the correct form of the verb **be** (**am**, **is**, or **are**).

1. You _____ standing on my foot.

2. I _____ going for a walk.

3. The firefighter _____ driving the engine.

4. Chandra and I _____ playing basketball.

5. The band _____ marching in the parade.

6. Denver _____ east of San Francisco.

7. My parents _____ in Hawaii.

8. Who _____ coming camping with me next weekend?

9. Julia and Ben _____ in third grade.

10. I _____ cooking potatoes and a pie for Thanksgiving.

11. You and Max _____ winning an award.

LANGUAGE ARTS

Skill 63: Subject-Verb Agreement

When a sentence has a singular subject, the verb ends with **s** or **es**.

Add **s** to most regular verbs that have a single subject.

Example: The *boat* sail**s** close to shore.

Add **es** to regular verbs that have a single subject and end in **sh**, **ch**, **s**, **x**, and **z**.

Example: *Gran* kiss**es** us good-bye.

When the subject is plural, the verb does not end with **s** or **es**.

Example: The *kittens* sleep on the sofa.

Directions: Read the paragraph below. Add or delete **s** or **es** from the verbs so that they agree with their subjects. Use this symbol (^) to add a letter or letters.

Mr. Huff wash his car on Saturdays. Adam and Amy help him. Mr. Huff sprays the car with warm water and soap. He scrub the car with a big sponge. The children clean the windshield and the mirrors. They use clean, soft rags. Adam wax the beautiful red car. It shine in the sunlight. Mr. Huff take Adam and Amy for a drive in the shiny car every Saturday afternoon. Then, they walk in the park.

Directions: Read each sentence below. Then, read the pair of verbs in parentheses ( ). Choose the correct verb form. Write it on the line.

1. Emily and Mateo _____ a ball in the backyard. (toss, tosses)

2. The Smiths _____ their pumpkins every autumn. (carve, carves)

3. My little brother _____ the dog with a new brush. (brush, brushes)

4. Brian _____ five miles a day when he is in training for a race. (run, runs)

5. The blender _____ the ingredients. (mix, mixes)

6. The Thompsons _____ near a snowy mountain every winter. (camp, camps)

7. The shaggy Irish setter _____ the ball each time I throw it. (catch, catches)

8. Grandma Stella _____ about one hour away. (live, lives)

LANGUAGE ARTS

A **helping verb** is a word used with an action verb.

Example: might, **shall**, and **are**

They **are** meeting us at noon. Harry **might** ask your opinion.

Directions: Finish each sentence with a helping verb from the Word Bank. The first one is done for you.

Word Bank			
can	could	must	might
may	would	should	will
shall	did	does	do
had	have	has	am
are	were	is	
be	being	been	

1. Tomorrow, I _____ might _____ play soccer.

2. Mom _____ buy my new dress tonight.

3. Yesterday, my new books _____ ripped by the cat.

4. I _____ going to ask my sister to go to the mall.

5. She usually _____ not like football.

6. But, she _____ go with me because I am her friend.

7. She _____ promised to watch the entire football game.

8. He _____ helped me with my homework.

9. I _____ spell a lot better because of his help.

10. Maybe I _____ finish the semester at the top of my class.

Common Helping Verbs

am	can	does	is	shall	will
are	could	had	may	should	would
be	did	has	might	was	
been	do	have	must	were	

Directions: Underline the action verb in each sentence. Then, choose the best helping verb and write it on the line.

1. Jasmine's family _____ organizing a neighborhood recycling project. (is had are)

2. They _____ talking to their neighbors.
   (is may are)

3. Mr. Chang's children _____ look for old newspapers and magazines. (will do were)

4. The Benson family _____ collecting plastic bottles.
   (should is did)

5. Jackie _____ open a lemonade stand to make some money. (have was might)

6. Mrs. Zane said she _____ drive us to the recycling center.
   (would be are)

7. We _____ respect our planet.
   (have must are)

LANGUAGE ARTS

The word **went** does not need a helping verb.

Examples: Correct: Matt **went** to the museum.

Incorrect: Matt **has went** to the museum.

The word **gone** does need a helping verb.

Examples: Correct: Matt **has gone** to the museum.

Incorrect: Matt **gone** to the museum.

Directions: Write **C** in the blank if the verb is used correctly. Write **X** in the blank if the verb is not used correctly.

1. _____ She has gone to my school since last year.

2. _____ He has gone to the park twice this week.

3. _____ He has went to the same dentist all year.

4. _____ I have went to that doctor since I was born.

5. _____ She is long gone!

6. _____ Who among us has not gone to get lunch yet?

7. _____ The family has gone on two camping trips this year.

8. _____ The class went on three field trips this year.

Directions: Write **C** in the blank if the verb is used correctly. Write **X** in the blank if the verb is not used correctly.

1. _____ Who has not went to the teacher with the correct answer?

2. _____ We have not went on our trip yet.

3. _____ Who has went for the food?

4. _____ The bus has gone to pick up the students.

5. _____ The family has gone to the movies.

6. _____ Have you went to visit the new bookstore?

7. _____ She has gone on and on about how funny you are!

8. _____ Garey has already went to the store.

9. _____ The train went through five cities.

10. _____ Lola and Bailey went to the pet store.

11. _____ Dr. Chen gone home for the day.

12. _____ We have went to the library every day.

LANGUAGE ARTS

A **present-tense** verb tells what is happening now, happens often, or is about to happen. If the subject is one noun or pronoun (**he**, **she**, or **it**), add an **s** to the verb.

Examples: The **bird** eat**s** the seeds.   **He** plant**s** a flower.
  She swing**s** high.   **It** look**s** like a worm.

If the subject is **I**, **you**, or more than one person, place, or thing, do not add an **s**.

Examples: **I** see a rainbow!   **Plants** grow in the sun.
  You rake the leaves.   **We** work hard.

Directions: Circle the form of the verb that matches the subject in each sentence.

1. I (like, likes) to plant the vegetables.

2. This carrot (taste, tastes) the best.

3. The crows (eat, eats) the corn.

4. The scarecrow (scare, scares) them away.

5. A teeny, tiny spider (crawl, crawls) on the vine.

6. It (move, moves) fast!

7. The yellow flowers (grow, grows) in the garden.

8. My sister (plant, plants) some seeds.

Directions: Rewrite each sentence, using the verb **is** and writing the **ing** form of the verb. The first one is done for you.

1. He cooks the cheeseburgers.

   He is cooking the cheeseburgers.

2. Sharon dances to that song.

   _____

3. Eric washed the boat.

   _____

4. Mr. Benson smiles at me.

   _____

Directions: Write a verb for each sentence below that tells something that is happening now. Use the verb **is** and the **ing** form of the verb. The first one is done for you.

1. The big, brown dog is barking_____.

2. The little baby _____.

3. The nine-year-old girl _____.

4. The monster on television _____.

5. Our old minivan _____.

LANGUAGE ARTS

When you write about something that already happened, add **ed** to most verbs. For some verbs that have a short vowel and end in one consonant, double the consonant before adding **ed**.

Examples: He hug**ged** his pillow.   The dog grab**bed** the stick.

To make many verbs past tense, add **ed**.

Examples: cook + ed = cooked   wish + ed = wished

When a verb ends in a **silent e**, add only **d**.

Examples: hope + ed = hoped

When a verb ends in **y** after a consonant, change the **y** to **i** and add **ed**.

Example: hurry + ed = hurried

When a verb ends in a single consonant after a single short vowel, double the final consonant before adding **ed**.

Example: stop + ed = stopped

Directions: Use the verb from the first sentence or clause to complete the second sentence. Change the verb in the second sentence to the past tense. Double the consonant and add **ed**. The first one is done for you.

1. We skip to school.

   Yesterday, we _____skipped_____ the whole way.

2. It is not nice to grab things.

   When you _____ my apple, I felt mad.

3. Did anyone hug you today?

   Mom _____ me this morning.

Directions: Use the verb from the first sentence or clause to complete the second sentence. Change the verb in the second sentence to the past tense. Double the consonant and add **ed**.

1. We plan our vacations every year.

   Last year, we _____ to go to the mountains.

2. Is it my turn to stir the pot?

   You _____ it last time.

3. Let's clap for Andy, just like we _____ for Amy.

Directions: Rewrite each verb in the past tense. The first one is done for you.

1. call _____called_____   2. copy _____

3. frown _____   4. smile _____

5. live _____   6. talk _____

7. name _____   8. list _____

9. spy _____   10. phone _____

11. bake _____   12. type _____

LANGUAGE ARTS

68: Future-Tense Verbs

The **future tense** of a verb tells about something that has not happened yet but will happen in the future. **Will** or **shall** are usually used with future tense.

Directions: Change the verb tense in each sentence to future tense. The first one is done for you.

1. She cooks dinner.

   She will cook dinner.

2. He plays soccer.

   _____

3. She bikes to the bank.

   _____

4. I remember to vote.

   _____

5. Jack mows the lawn every week.

   _____

6. We go on vacation soon.

   _____

Directions: On the line, write **PA** if a sentence takes place in the past. Write **PR** if it takes place in the present. Then, rewrite each sentence in the future tense.

Example: __PA__ The play ended at 9:00.

The play will end at 9:00.

1. _____ The dog barked at the loud truck.

_____

2. _____ The gardener picks flowers from her wildflower garden.

_____

3. _____ The frog pulls a worm from the pond.

_____

4. _____ A ladybug landed on Layla's shoulder.

_____

Directions: Write a sentence about somewhere you will go or something you will do in the future. Underline the verb.

_____

LANGUAGE ARTS

A word that **describes** a noun is called an **adjective**.

Adjectives tell:

What Kind:	**white** egg	**small** car	**messy** room
How Many:	**five** flags	**many** books	**a half-dozen** donuts
Which One:	**those** ducklings	**that** lamp	**this** bowl

Directions: Write an adjective that could describe each thing.

1. cereal _____

2. shoes _____

3. cat _____

4. test _____

5. boys _____

6. frog _____

7. sisters _____

8. bikes _____

9. ice cream _____

LANGUAGE ARTS

Skill 69: Adjectives

Directions: Finish each sentence using an adjective from the Word Bank.

Word Bank

green   soft   ugly   expensive   thousands   warty

1. The _____ pillows were very _____

   to buy because they were made of _____ of downy

   feathers.

2. The _____, _____ frog was so

   _____ that everybody was afraid to look at him.

Directions: Finish each sentence using an adjective from the Word Bank.

Word Bank

hungry   beautiful   delicate   tall   loud   scary

1. Brown bears can be very _____ when they are

   _____. They stand up _____ and let

   out _____ growls.

2. Tulips are _____ flowers and quite

   _____. Their petals feel like smooth velvet.

Skill 70: Comparative Adjectives and Adverbs

Add the suffix **er** to an adjective to compare two things.

Example: My feet are **large**.

Your feet are **larger** than my feet.

When a one-syllable adjective ends in a single consonant and the vowel is short, double the final consonant before adding **er**. When a word ends in two or more consonants, add **er**.

Examples: big — bigger (single consonant)

bold — bolder (two consonants)

When an adjective ends in **y**, change the **y** to **i** before adding **er**.

Example: easy — easier

Add the suffix **est** to adjectives to compare more than two things.

Example: My glass is **full**.   Your glass is **fuller**.   His glass is **fullest**.

When a one-syllable adjective ends in a single consonant and the vowel sound is short, double the final consonant before adding **est**.

Examples: big — biggest (short vowel)

steep — steepest (long vowel)

When an adjective ends in **y**, change the **y** to **i** before adding **est**.

Example: easy — easiest

Directions: Use the correct rule to add **er** to the words below for numbers 1–4. Then, use the correct rule to add **est** to the words below for numbers 5–8.

1. fast _____

2. thin _____

3. long _____

4. clean _____

5. pretty _____

6. early _____

7. quick _____

8. trim _____

Skill 70: Comparative Adjectives and Adverbs

To make a comparison using adverbs that end in **ly**, use the words *more* or *most*.

Example: Dawn read the book *more slowly* than Kim.

My sister sang *most beautifully* of all the girls in her class.

Directions: Fill in the spaces in the chart with the correct adverbs. Remember that some comparative adverbs need to be used with the words *more* or *most*.

slowly	_____	most slowly
fast	faster	_____
skillfully	_____	_____
happily	more happily	_____
_____	more patiently	most patiently
_____	_____	latest
safely	_____	most safely
playfully	_____	_____

fast   faster   fastest

Skill 71: Adverbs

Like adjectives, **adverbs** are describing words. They describe verbs. Adverbs tell **how**, **when**, or **where** the action takes place.

Examples:	**How**	**When**	**Where**
	slowly	yesterday	here
	gracefully	today	there
	swiftly	tomorrow	everywhere
	quickly	soon	

To identify an adverb, locate the verb, then ask yourself if there are any words that tell how, when, or where the action takes place.

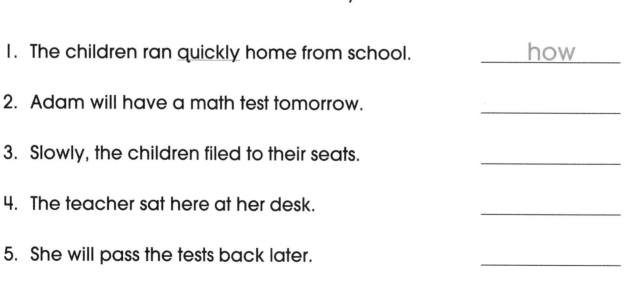

Directions: Underline the adverb in each sentence. Then, write whether it tells **how**, **when**, or **where**. The first one is done for you

1. The children ran <u>quickly</u> home from school. _____how_____

2. Adam will have a math test tomorrow. _____

3. Slowly, the children filed to their seats. _____

4. The teacher sat here at her desk. _____

5. She will pass the tests back later. _____

6. The students received their grades happily. _____

Directions: Use an **adverb** from the Word Bank to finish each sentence. Make sure the adverb you choose makes sense with the rest of the sentence.

Word Bank			
loudly	here	carefully	carelessly
inside	slowly	below	everywhere

1. Zach left the library book

   _____.

2. We looked _____ for his jacket.

3. We will have recess _____ because it is raining.

4. From the top of the mountain, we could see the village far

   _____.

5. We watched the turtle move _____ across the yard.

6. Everyone completed the math test _____.

7. The fire was caused by someone _____ tossing a match.

8. The alarm rang _____ while we were eating.

LANGUAGE ARTS

149

Skill 72: Articles

A, **an**, and **the** are called **articles**.

A and **an** introduce singular nouns. Use **a** when the next word begins with a consonant sound. Use **an** when the next word begins with a vowel sound.

Examples: a chair   **an** antelope

The introduces both singular and plural nouns.

Examples: the beaver   **the** flowers

Directions: Underline the correct article for each word.

1. (the, an)   field
2. (a, an)   award
3. (an, the)   ball
4. (a, the)   wheels
5. (a, an)   inning
6. (an, the)   sticks
7. (the, a)   goalposts
8. (a, an)   obstacle
9. (a, an)   umpire
10. (an, the)   quarterback

11. (a, an) oven
12. (an, the) oranges
13. (the, a) cities
14. (an, a) elephant
15. (a, the) igloo
16. (a, an) nest
17. (an, a) ape
18. (the, an) staircase
19. (a, the) highways
20. (a, an) yo-yo

Directions: Write **a** or **an** in each sentence below. The first one is done for you.

1. My bike had _____a_____ flat tire.

2. They brought _____ goat to the farm.

3. My mom wears _____ old pair of shoes to mow the lawn.

4. We had _____ party for my grandfather.

5. Everybody had _____ lemonade after the game.

6. We bought _____ picnic table for our backyard.

7. We saw _____ cat sleeping in the shade.

8. It was _____ evening to be remembered.

9. Karina gave _____ balloon to her brother.

10. It was _____ amazing day!

11. The park had _____ old merry-go-round.

12. Our grandpa gave each of us _____ dollar.

LANGUAGE ARTS

Words that combine sentences or ideas, such as **and**, **but**, **or**, **because**, **when**, **after**, and **so**, are called **conjunctions**.

Examples: I played soccer, **and** Tom played volleyball.

She likes apples, **but** I do not.

We could play music **or** just enjoy the silence.

I needed the computer **because** I had to write a book report.

He gave me the letter **when** I asked for it.

I asked her to eat lunch **after** she finished the test.

You wanted my skateboard, **so** I gave it to you.

Using different conjunctions can affect the meaning of a sentence.

Example: He gave me the money **when** I asked for it.

He gave me the money **after** I asked for it.

Directions: Choose the best conjunction to combine each pair of sentences. The first one is done for you.

1. I like my hair brown. Mom likes my hair blond.

   I like my hair brown, but Mom likes it blond.

2. I can remember what she looks like. I can't remember her name.

   _____

3. We will have to wash the dishes. We won't have clean plates for dinner.

   _____

4. Sam plays the drums. Aiden plays the trumpet.

   _____

LANGUAGE ARTS

Directions: Combine each pair of sentences using a conjunction. There may be more than one correct answer for each item.

1. Jack wants to go swimming and camping. His sister has been doing both every summer for years.

   _____

   _____

2. Dion enjoys watching soccer. He hasn't started playing yet.

   _____

   _____

3. Jade can buy a drum set. She can buy new clothes for school.

   _____

   _____

4. James scored a goal. Everyone cheered, clapped, and yelled.

   _____

   _____

5. Amanda noticed the crack. She picked up her glass.

   _____

   _____

LANGUAGE ARTS

A **statement** is a sentence that tells something.

Directions: Use the words in the Word Bank to complete the statements below.

Word Bank

glue	share
decide	take
count	fold

1. It took two minutes for Kate to _____ the money.

2. Ben wants to _____ his cake with me.

3. "I can't _____ which pillow to choose," said Micah.

4. _____ can be used to make things stick together.

5. "This is how you _____ your paper in half," said Mrs. Smith.

6. The opposite of **give** is _____.

Directions: Write a statement on the line.

_____

_____

_____

Directions: Read the sentences below. Put an **X** on the line after each sentence that is a statement.

1. It is simple and fun to make your own paint. _____

2. Buy some ice cream tomorrow. _____

3. We made twenty dollars selling our used books. _____

4. Stir in the salt until it dissolves. _____

5. Use a juicer to squeeze the oranges. _____

6. We bought napkins and cups. _____

7. Jessica will be ten in October. _____

8. Add some ice to your drink. _____

9. Astronauts are planning a mission to Mars. _____

10. Each muffin contains a teaspoon of sugar. _____

11. Please have a seat. _____

12. Nobody knew how long the trip would take. _____

LANGUAGE ARTS

Skill 75: Commands

A **command** is a sentence that tells someone to do something.

Directions: Use a word from the Word Bank to finish each command below.

Word Bank

glue	share
decide	enter
add	fold

1. _____ a cup of flour to the cookie batter.

2. _____ how much time you will need to write your report.

3. Please _____ the picture of the cat onto the paper.

4. _____ through this door and leave through the other door.

5. Please _____ the letter and put it into an envelope.

6. _____ your toys with your sister.

Directions: Write a command.

_____

_____

_____

Directions: Read the sentences below. Put an **X** on the line after each sentence that is a command.

1. Wash your clothes. _____

2. The refrigerator was full for the party. _____

3. We walked to the park for a picnic. _____

4. Please do not talk so loudly. _____

5. I had to rewrite my report. _____

6. The movie preview was interesting. _____

7. Don't be late. _____

8. Sam loves to play in the snow. _____

9. Start your homework before dinner. _____

10. Nine o'clock is too late to play outside. _____

11. Zip your coat and put on a hat. _____

12. Our dogs don't like to be inside. _____

LANGUAGE ARTS

Questions are asking sentences. They begin with a capital letter and end with a question mark. Many questions begin with the words **who**, **what**, **why**, **when**, **where**, or **how**.

Directions: Write six questions using the question words below. Make sure to end each question with a question mark.

1. Who

   _____

2. What

   _____

3. Why

   _____

4. When

   _____

5. Where

   _____

6. How

   _____

100 Third Grade Skills

Skill 76: Questions

Directions: Read the sentences below. Then, rewrite them as questions.

1. The largest frog in the world is called the Goliath frog.

   _____

   _____

2. The skin of a toad feels dry and bumpy.

   _____

   _____

3. Gliding leaf frogs can glide almost 50 feet in the air.

   _____

   _____

4. The poison dart frog lives in Columbia, South America.

   _____

   _____

5. There are more than 4,000 species of frogs in the world.

   _____

   _____

LANGUAGE ARTS

Skill 77: Exclamations

Exclamations are sentences that show excitement or surprise.

Example: Wait! or **Don't forget to call!**

Directions: Add an exclamation point at the end of each sentence or phrase that expresses strong feelings. Add a period at the end of each statement.

1. My parents and I were watching television

2. The snow began falling around noon

3. I couldn't believe my eyes

4. The snow was really coming down

5. We turned the television off and looked out the window

6. The snow looked like a white blanket

7. How beautiful

8. We decided to put on our coats and go outside

9. We would build the best snowman ever

Skill 77: Exclamations

Directions: Add an exclamation point at the end of each sentence or phrase that expresses strong feelings. Add a period at the end of each statement.

1. Look out

2. The cat needs to go to the vet

3. Wait for me

4. We won the soccer tournament

5. I lost my phone

6. Ella is eight

7. My grandma had 16 brothers and sisters

8. Harry wore a new suit to the wedding

9. The store was filled with shoppers

10. Look at that

11. It rained last night

LANGUAGE ARTS

Skill 78: Parts of a Sentence: Subjects

The **subject** of a sentence is what a sentence is about. In a statement, the subject is usually found at the beginning of the sentence before the verb. A subject can be a single word, or it can be several words.

Examples: **The entire team** cheered when the winning goal was scored.

Irina loves to eat oatmeal for breakfast.

Directions: Underline the subject in each sentence below.

1. The brave firefighters are always ready to go.

2. A loud bell rings.

3. They slide down a tall pole.

4. One person drives the truck.

5. The siren is very loud.

6. We see the truck go by our school.

7. A dog runs after the truck.

8. It stops at an old, empty house.

Directions: Use your own words to write the subject in each sentence below.

  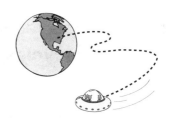

1. _____ landed in my backyard.

2. _____ rushed out of the house.

3. _____ had bright lights.

4. _____ were tall and green.

5. _____ talked to me.

6. _____ came outside with me.

7. _____ ran into the house.

8. _____ shook hands.

9. _____ said funny things.

10. _____ gave us a ride.

11. _____ flew away.

12. _____ will come back soon.

LANGUAGE ARTS

Skill 79: Parts of a Sentence: Predicates

The **predicate** of a sentence tells what the subject is doing. The predicate contains the action, linking, and/or helping verb. The verb is usually the first word of the predicate.

Examples: Noel recycles all his cans and bottles.
Recycles all his cans and bottles is the predicate.

Directions: Underline the predicate in each sentence. The first one has been done for you.

1. The choir sang joyfully.

2. Their song had both high and low notes.

3. Sal played the guitar while they sang.

4. This Saturday, the band will have a concert in the park.

5. John is working hard on his report.

6. He will write a report on electricity.

7. The report will tell about Thomas Jefferson.

8. Laura and Misty played on the slide.

Directions: Write a predicate for each subject to make a complete sentence.

1. The busy mall _____

2. The restaurants _____

3. The children _____

4. Mom _____

5. The baby _____

Directions: Underline the predicate in each sentence. The first one is done for you.

1. The busy editor <u>wrote a page about subjects and predicates.</u>

2. She was hopeful the children would understand sentences.

3. The children completed their assignment quickly.

4. They went outside.

5. The teacher watched the boys play ball.

LANGUAGE ARTS

Skill 80: Sentence Fragments

A **sentence** is a group of words that expresses a complete thought. It contains a subject and a predicate.

Example: Luna eats tacos every day.

A **sentence fragment** does not express a complete thought. It may be missing either the subject or the predicate.

Example: Lettuce and salsa on it.

Directions: Read each group of words. Circle **S** if it is a sentence. Circle **F** if it is a fragment.

1. Tacos taste delicious.	S	F
2. Let the tortillas cool down.	S	F
3. Cheese in the refrigerator.	S	F
4. Anthony pours salsa on the tortillas.	S	F
5. Mom puts the radishes on the tortillas.	S	F
6. Sprinkled on top.	S	F
7. Everyone eats happily.	S	F

Skill 80: Sentence Fragments

Directions: Read each group of words. Circle **S** if it is a sentence. Circle **F** if it is a fragment.

1. Mario sprinkles the tacos with cilantro.   S   F

2. More tomatoes.   S   F

3. We bake the tacos in the oven for 10 minutes.   S   F

4. Served hot.   S   F

5. Add avocado.   S   F

Directions: Write three sentences of your own about tacos. Each sentence needs a subject and a predicate.

1. _____

_____

2. _____

_____

3. _____

_____

LANGUAGE ARTS

Skill 81: Run-On Sentences

A **run-on sentence** occurs when two or more sentences are joined together without punctuation.

Examples: **Run-on sentence:** I lost my way once did you?

Two sentences with correct punctuation: I lost my way once. Did you?

Directions: Rewrite the run-on sentences correctly with periods, exclamation points, or question marks. The first one is done for you.

1. Did you take my umbrella I can't find it anywhere!

    Did you take my umbrella? I can't find it anywhere!

2. How can you stand that song I can't!

    _____

3. The cake is gone I see only crumbs.

    _____

4. The cats were meowing they were hungry.

    _____

5. The clouds came up we knew the storm would hit soon.

    _____

Skill 81: Run-On Sentences

Directions: Read each item below. If it is a complete sentence, write **C** on the line. If it is a run-on sentence, write **R** on the line.

1. Jackson caught the ball did you see that? _____

2. The tide was high the waves crashed on the shore. _____

3. The team was excited they won they cheered, clapped, and yelled. _____

4. Andrew ran five miles. _____

5. The ball bounced off the ground. _____

6. We hiked up the mountain. _____

7. If you have time, please make dinner. _____

8. I helped Sam wash his car it was dirty from the storm. _____

9. Charlotte was looking forward to seeing the baby dolphins with their mothers. _____

10. I ran five miles it was challenging! _____

A **compound subject** is a subject with two parts joined by the word **and** or another conjunction. The subjects share the same predicate.

Example:

Simple Subjects: Her shoes were covered with mud.
Her ankles were covered with mud, too.

Compound Subject: Her shoes and ankles were covered with mud.

The predicate in both sentences is **were covered with mud**.

If sentences do not share the same predicate, they cannot be combined to form one sentence with a compound subject.

Example: Mary laughed at the story.
Tanya laughed at the television show.

The predicates **laughed at the story** and **laughed at the television show** are not the same. The sentences cannot be combined to form one sentence with a compound subject.

Directions: Combine each pair of sentences into one sentence with a compound subject.

1. Bill coughed. Kassie coughed.

   _____

2. Kristin made dinner. Joey made dinner.

   _____

3. Fruit flies are insects. Ladybugs are insects.

   _____

LANGUAGE ARTS

Skill 82: Compound Subjects

Directions: Combine each pair of sentences into one sentence with a compound subject.

1. The girls are planning a picnic. The boys are planning a picnic.

   _____

2. Our dog ran after the squirrel. Our cat ran after the squirrel.

   _____

3. Joshua got lost in the woods. Daniel got lost in the woods.

   _____

4. Pete loves running. Jake loves running.

   _____

5. A cat scratched Elizabeth. A dog scratched Elizabeth.

   _____

6. Sharon is smiling. Susan is smiling.

   _____

7. The boys have nice clothes. The girls have nice clothes.

   _____

Skill 83: Compound Sentences

A simple sentence has a subject and a predicate. A **compound sentence** is made up of two simple sentences. They are joined by a comma and a conjunction, such as **or**, **and**, or **but**.

simple   Kevin made the salad.
              Moni cooked the pizza.

compound   Kevin made the salad, **and** Moni cooked the pizza.

Directions: Read each sentence. If the sentence is a compound sentence, circle the comma and the conjunction.

1. Marleen pops a balloon, and Eric jumps.

2. All the presents were under the tree.

3. Kiko rides a bike.

4. Sabrina plays soccer, but Adam writes a poem.

5. The cake is chocolate, and the ice cream is vanilla.

6. Kris may dance alone, or everyone could dance together.

7. Mother tells everyone to come inside.

8. Claire opens her presents, and Ali reads the cards.

Skill 83: Compound Sentences

Directions: Combine the simple sentences to make a compound sentence. Use a comma and a conjunction.

1. Sheila wears roller skates. Andy rides a skateboard.

   _____

2. The children play in the park. The adults watch.

   _____

3. Seth buys hamburgers. Karen prefers sandwiches.

   _____

4. Swimming is fun. It is not allowed in this lake.

   _____

5. My mom flies a kite. My dad unpacks the lunch basket.

   _____

6. You can eat a banana. You can eat an apple.

   _____

7. We wanted to ride the bumper cars. It was too late.

   _____

LANGUAGE ARTS

Skill **84**: Combining Repeated Words

You can combine two shorter sentences into one longer sentence by eliminating words that are repeated.

Example: Dawn cleared snow from the front yard.
Dawn cleared snow with a new shovel.
Dawn cleared snow from the front yard with a new shovel.

Directions: Underline the repeated words and write a combined sentence.

1. I rode around Big Bear Lake. I rode on a horse.

   _____

2. We are planning a Halloween party for our friends. We are planning a Halloween party next Saturday.

   _____

   _____

3. My dad served steaming hot pasta. My dad served pasta on a large platter.

   _____

4. I ran errands for for my grandma today. I ran errands because she was sick.

   _____

5. The children saw fresh footprints in the mud. They saw fresh footprints under the window.

   _____

Directions: Underline the repeated words and write a combined sentence.

1. I hiked up the hill in the snow. I hiked up the hill in my new boots.

   _____

   _____

2. Jake took his cat to the vet yesterday. Jake took his cat to the vet because she was sick.

   _____

   _____

3. My cousin baked delicious cookies for the party. My cousin baked delicious cookies in her new oven.

   _____

   _____

4. Andrew put the pillows in the tent for his family. Andrew put the pillows in the tent and unrolled the sleeping bags.

   _____

   _____

5. I washed my dad's car last night. I washed my dad's car because he was too busy.

   _____

   _____

LANGUAGE ARTS

85: Capitalizing the First Word in a Sentence and "I"

The first word in a sentence should begin with a capital letter. The name of a person begins with a capital letter. The pronoun **I** is written as a capital letter.

Directions: Read each sentence. Use three short lines to underline the first letter of each word that needs a capital letter. Rewrite the word correctly. The first one is done for you.

1. _____Today_____ today is the first day of school.

2. _____ i take the bus to school.

3. _____ Jamie and i play soccer at recess.

4. _____ everyone has to write a story about something fun they did over the summer.

5. _____ i finished my science experiment.

6. _____ lunch is served at 11:30.

7. _____ our principal came to visit our class.

8. _____ Sam and i were quiet in the library.

9. _____ the teacher writes the homework on the board.

10. _____ i cleaned my desk before I went home.

11. _____ have a great day.

Skill 85: Capitalizing the First Word in a Sentence and "I"

Directions: Read each sentence. Use three short lines to underline the first letter of each word that needs a capital letter. Rewrite each sentence correctly. The first one is done for you.

1. The librarian helped tracy find a book about susan b. anthony.

   The librarian helped Tracy find a book about Susan B. Anthony.

2. i learned that george washington was the first president. _____

   _____

3. matt and i are writing a report about john f. kennedy. _____

   _____

4. elisa and i are studying about samuel adams. _____

   _____

5. harriet tubman helped rescue many people from slavery. _____

   _____

6. Many people admire helen keller's courage and intelligence.

   _____

   _____

7. Can i write a report about jackie robinson? _____

   _____

LANGUAGE ARTS

Capitalize the **specific names of people and pets**.

Examples: My cousin **Peter** moved here from Germany.
We named the kitten **Zorro**.

A **title** that comes before a name is capitalized.

Examples: Grandpa Bruce   **President** Abraham Lincoln

Titles of respect are also capitalized.

Examples: Dr. Gupta   **Mrs.** Cohen

If a title is not used with a name, it is not capitalized.

Directions: Complete each sentence below with the words in parentheses ( ). Some of the words will need to be capitalized. Others will not.

1. Kelly took her dog, _____, for a walk to the park. (abby)

2. My school has a new _____. (teacher)

3. On Saturday, _____ is coming to visit. (grandpa)

4. The best teacher I ever had was _____. (mr. benham)

5. The baby panda at the zoo is named _____. (mica)

Skill **86**: Capitalizing Names and Titles

Directions: Write the words in the correct column with capital letters at the beginning of each word. Use the words in the word box.

president barack obama	rover
mr. hoffer	uncle brian
grandma stella	spot
judge hommell	dr. kosten
captain albertson	ace

people   **people with titles**   **pets**

LANGUAGE ARTS

The **days of the week** each begin with a capital letter.

Examples: Monday, Tuesday, Wednesday

The **months of the year** are capitalized.

Examples: January, February, March

The **names of holidays** are capitalized.

Examples: Memorial Day, Mother's Day

Directions: Complete the sentences below with the name of a day, month, or holiday. Remember to use capital letters where needed.

1. I was born in the month of _____.

2. On _____, many people stay up until midnight to welcome the new year.

3. On _____, Austin made a card for his dad and washed his dad's car.

4. _____ is the middle of the week.

5. The groundhog did not see his shadow on _____ this year.

6. Independence Day is on _____ 4th every year.

Skill 87: Capitalizing Dates and Holidays

Directions: Write the words in the correct columns with capital letters at the beginning of each word. Use the words in the word box.

saturday	december
thanksgiving	friday
october	christmas
kwanzaa	wednesday
arbor day	july

days	**months**	**holidays**

Directions: Write two sentences that include a holiday, month, or day of the week.

1. _____

_____

2. _____

_____

Skill 88: Capitalizing Book, Movie, and Song Titles

The titles of books, movies, and songs are capitalized. Small words, like **of**, **the**, **and**, **in**, **to**, **a**, **an**, and **from**, do not begin with a capital letter unless they are the first or last word of a title.

Books	Movies	Songs
<u>Where the Sidewalk Ends</u>	<u>The Parent Trap</u>	"Hakuna Matata"

Directions: Rewrite the sentences below. Capitalize the names of books, movies, and song titles.

1. It took Shakhil only two days to read the book <u>twilight</u>.

   _____

   _____

2. Sara is sleeping over tonight, and we are going to watch <u>star wars</u>.

   _____

   _____

3. I love the poems in Emily Dickinson's book <u>poetry all kids should know</u>.

   _____

   _____

4. If you watch Schoolhouse Rock, you can learn the song "verb: that's what's happening."

   _____

   _____

Directions: Write the books, movies, and song titles in the correct columns. Use the word box. Make sure to add capital letters.

"we wish you a merry christmas"	ivy and bean
tales of a fourth grade nothing	the nightmare before christmas
the neverending story	"yellow submarine"
amelia hits the road	frozen
"let it go"	toy story

books	movies	song titles

Directions: Write two sentences that include a book, movie, or song title.

1. _____

   _____

2. _____

   _____

LANGUAGE ARTS

Skill 89: Capitalizing Place Names

The **names of specific places** always begin with a capital letter.

Examples: Madison, **Wisconsin**   **Italy**   **Liberty Avenue**

Directions: Complete each sentence below with the word or words in parentheses ( ). Remember to capitalize the names of specific places.

1. There are many towns across _____ (america) that have interesting names.

2. Have you ever heard of Frankenstein, _____ (missouri)?

3. Some towns are named after foods, like _____

   _____ (avocado, california).

4. Some names, like Chickasawhatchee and _____ (goochland) are fun to say.

5. A person from _____ (germany) might be surprised to find a town named Berlin in Ohio.

6. If you're on your way to visit _____ (mount rushmore), look for Igloo, South Dakota.

7. The town of Boring, _____ (oregon), has been paired with Dull, Scotland, to promote tourism.

Directions: Rewrite the sentences using correct capitalization.

1. Take wilbur street to preston parkway and turn left.

   _____

2. Travel about two miles on preston parkway.

   _____

3. You will pass montgomery library and the talbot recreation center.

   _____

   _____

4. At the light, turn right onto solomon road.

   _____

5. You will drive over haystack bridge and pass a gas station.

   _____

6. children's playhouse is located on the west side of the street.

   _____

7. The address is 1548 solomon road.

   _____

LANGUAGE ARTS

Periods, Question Marks, and Exclamation Points

A statement ends with a **period** (.).

A question ends with a **question mark** (?).

A command ends with a **period** (.).

An exclamation ends with an **exclamation point** (!).

Directions: Write the correct punctuation mark in each box.

1. Every Saturday morning, we help a senior citizen ☐

2. Would you like to help us this Saturday ☐

3. Be at my house at 8:00 ☐

4. You can help me gather the supplies we will need ☐

5. I won't be late ☐

6. Today we are raking Mrs. Ray's yard ☐

7. That elm tree is huge ☐

8. Take these lawn bags to Bob and Eric ☐

9. What time will your dad pick us up ☐

Skill 90: Periods, Question Marks, and Exclamation Points

Directions: Write the correct punctuation mark in each box.

1. Tell Jan and Pat to mow the backyard ☐

2. Will you help them rake the backyard ☐

3. Don't mow too close to the flowers ☐

4. Look at that big gazebo ☐

5. Mrs. Ray has left lemonade there for us ☐

6. I will mow the front yard ☐

7. Will you sweep the front walks ☐

8. How long do you think that will take ☐

9. Go ask Mrs. Ray to come see her clean yard ☐

10. She thinks the yard looks super ☐

11. What will we do next Saturday ☐

12. Maybe Mr. Martinez will hire us ☐

LANGUAGE ARTS

Skill 91: Commas with Dates, Cities, States, and Addresses

Commas are used in dates. They are used in between the day and the year.

Example: September 22, 2015

Commas are also used in between the names of cities and states or cities and countries.

Example: Paris, France

In an address, a comma is used between the city name and state abbreviation.

Example: Juneau, AK

Directions: Read the sentences below. Add commas where they are needed.

1. The Rock and Roll Hall of Fame is in Cleveland Ohio.

2. Basketball star LeBron James was born on December 30 1984.

3. Sarah Hughes skated in the Winter Olympics in Salt Lake City Utah.

4. Abby Wambach grew up in Rochester NY, and later became a star soccer player.

5. Olympic swimmer Michael Phelps was born in Baltimore Maryland, in 1985.

Skill 91: Commas with Dates, Cities, States, and Addresses

Directions: Add commas where they are needed. Then, answer the questions.

1. October 12 2011

2. Amarillo Texas

3. Paris France

4. July 24 1974

5. San Diego CA

6. We drove from Portland Oregon, to Seattle Washington.

7. March 31 2016

8. New York NY

9. Athens Greece

10. April 2 2007

11. In what city and state were you born? _____

12. What is your birthdate? _____

Skill 92: Commas in a Series

A **series** is a list of words. Use a comma after each word in a series except the last word. Use a conjunction (**and**, **or**) before the last word in a series.

Examples: My family includes my **mom, dad, sister, and me**.
Fruit, cookies, or popcorn are our snack choices today.

Directions: Add commas to these sentences.

1. We are going on a trip to Germany Prague and France.

2. My mother father sister and I are packing our suitcases.

3. I need to pack my shampoo toothpaste and lotion.

4. Mom, I can't find my shirt pants or gloves!

5. I can take my blue jeans green shorts and purple socks.

6. Do I need tennis shoes nice shoes or boots?

7. A magazine a book and music are also good things to pack.

8. Mom tucks me in kisses me and tells me good night.

9. Mom turns out the lights in my room the hall and the stairs.

10. I can't wait to travel play and have fun!

Skill 92: Commas in a Series

Directions: Read each paragraph. Add commas where they are needed.

An octopus is a strange ominous soft animal. An octopus has no bones can fit into very small places and in order to hide, it can change the color of its skin. They are carnivorous marine animals have large heads and mouths with strong beaks. An octopus swims by pushing water out of its body in the same way a jet engine works. An octopus is truly a unique animal.

A little young and curious octopus named Oscar lived in a small cave at the bottom of a beautiful blue sea. One day, Oscar was looking for something to eat when he saw a strange object. He took a closer look. He found a small strange and curious opening on one end and a big space in the middle, just like his cave. When Oscar squeezed in, he could see through the walls to the outside. There was an odd unique and puzzling pattern on the side of the cave that looked like this: COLA. Oscar didn't mind the strange pattern. He liked his new home.

A **simple sentence** tells about one complete thought. A **compound sentence** is made of two or more simple sentences. To form a compound sentence, use a comma and the conjunction **and**, **or**, or **but** to join the simple sentences.

The underlined parts of the compound sentence below can stand alone as simple sentences.

Example: <u>Do you want to go to the zoo</u>, **or** <u>would you rather go to the art museum?</u>

Directions: Read each sentence below. If it is a simple sentence, write **S** on the line. If it is a compound sentence, write **C**.

1. _____ Have you noticed snakes in your yard or your neighborhood?

2. _____ Feeding birds can be fun, and it can be educational.

3. _____ Some cats like feather toys, but others like catnip.

4. _____ Food placed on the ground will attract birds, but it will also attract other animals.

5. _____ Squirrels are known for eating bird food and scaring birds away.

6. _____ Once stray animals notice that you are feeding them, they will come to visit often.

Skill 93: Commas in Compound Sentences

Directions: Read the paragraph. Add commas where they are needed. Then, complete the exercise after the paragraphs.

The leaves of the poison ivy plant are shaped like almonds and they come in groups of three. Poison ivy can cause a rash and it can make you itch. The leaves of the plant contain oil that causes the rash. Some people can touch the plant but they will not get a rash.

The oil can stick to your clothes. Washing with soap and water can get rid of the oil and it can keep the rash from spreading. However, the best defense against poison ivy rash is to stay away from plants with leaves in groups of three.

Directions: Write a compound sentence about what you like to do and what a friend likes to do. Join the two parts of your sentence with a comma and the word **and** or **but**.

_____

_____

_____

_____

94: Punctuating Dialogue and Titles

Titles of books, movies, and plays are underlined.

Example: Lucas did a book report on <u>Two Heads Are Better Than One</u>.

Titles of songs, poems, and stories are set in quotation marks.

Example: Judith Viorst wrote the poem "If I Were in Charge of the World."

Directions: Read each sentence below. Underline the titles of books, movies, and plays. Put quotation marks around the titles of songs, stories, and poems.

1. Before soccer games, someone always sings The Star Spangled Banner.

2. Scotty Smalls is the main character in the movie The Sandlot.

3. My favorite poem is Eletelephony by Laura E. Richards.

4. Camden Little Theater is producing the play The Selfish Giant.

5. Laura Ingalls Wilder wrote Little House in the Big Woods.

6. The movie The Incredibles won an award for Best Animated Film.

7. Mira named her story A Day in the Life of a Horse.

8. Singing the song Purple People Eater makes my sister laugh.

94: Punctuating Dialogue and Titles

The exact words a person says are called **dialogue**. Quotation marks are used with dialogue.

Example: "My piano recital is on Saturday."

Directions: The sentences below are missing commas, periods, and quotation marks. Rewrite each sentence. Add punctuation marks where needed.

1. I have never been to a city before replied Audrey

   _____

2. Neither have I replied Chris

   _____

3. My cousin's city has huge buildings museums and restaurants said Jackson

   _____

   _____

4. He added I stay with them every fall, and there is always something to do

   _____

   _____

5. I would love to learn how to ride the subway and call a cab said Audrey

   _____

   _____

LANGUAGE ARTS

Skill 95: Contractions

A **contraction** is a shortened form of two words. An apostrophe shows where letters are missing.

Example: It is — It's

Directions: Write the words that are used in each contraction.

we're _____ + _____   they'll _____ + _____

you'll _____ + _____   aren't _____ + _____

I'm _____ + _____   isn't _____ + _____

Directions: Write the contraction for the two words shown.

you have _____   have not _____

had not _____   we will _____

they are _____   he is _____

she had _____   it will _____

I am _____   is not _____

Directions: Write a contraction that completes each sentence.

1. _____ going to be late for school.

2. You _____ have to wait for me.

3. They _____ coming to visit us this year.

4. We _____ go that way or _____ get lost again.

5. _____ Kim and Jesse be here by now?

6. We _____ ready for class to begin.

7. _____ they already spent too much money?

8. _____ wait for you at the airport.

9. _____ beautiful outside today!

10. _____ Kyle coming with us?

11. The announcer _____ pronounce my name right.

12. _____ be happy when I tell you the news.

A **contraction** is made up of two words that are shortened and put together to make one word. An **apostrophe** takes the place of the missing letters.

Examples: does not — doesn't   cannot — can't

Directions: Draw a line from each pair of words to its matching contraction.

1. is not		weren't
2. are not		wasn't
3. was not		aren't
4. were not		isn't
5. have not		didn't
6. can not		haven't
7. do not		couldn't
8. did not		can't
9. could not		shouldn't
10. should not		don't

Do not use a contraction that ends in **n't** with another negative, such as **no**, **nothing**, **no one**, and **never**.

Incorrect: I didn't get **no** milk.   **Correct:** I didn't get **any** milk.

Directions: Rewrite each sentence correctly.

1. Molly doesn't have no math classes.

_____

2. We aren't doing nothing for Spring Break.

_____

Apostrophes (') show ownership. Write **'s** at the end of a single person, place, or thing to show ownership.

Example: Mary's cat

Directions: Add **'s** to show ownership. The first one is done for you.

1. Jill's bike is broken.

2. That is Holly   flower garden.

3. Mark   new skates are black and green.

4. Mom threw away Dad   old shirt.

5. Buster   food dish was lost in the snowstorm.

6. The bunny   toy is broken.

7. The house   windows are dark.

8. I ate all of my sister   lunch.

9. Caleb   shoe has a hole in it.

10. The book   cover was interesting.

11. I am not sure where Mom   car is parked.

LANGUAGE ARTS

199

Negative words are words like **no**, **none**, **never**, **nothing**, **nobody**, **nowhere**, and **no one**. The word **not** and contractions that use **not** are also negative words. A sentence needs only one negative word. It is incorrect to use a **double negative**, or more than one negative word, in a sentence.

Example: **Correct:**   There were **not** any oranges in the refrigerator.
There were **no** oranges in the refrigerator.
Incorrect: There were **not no** oranges in the refrigerator.

Directions: Read each sentence. Circle the word or words from the pair in parentheses ( ) that correctly complete each sentence.

1. The jellyfish don't (never, ever) stop moving.

2. They don't do (anything, nothing) but follow the sun across the lake all day long.

3. My aunt said there (is, is not) nowhere on Earth she would rather go snorkeling.

4. People who swim with the jellyfish shouldn't (ever, never) lift or throw the delicate animals.

5. There aren't (no, any) jellyfish without stingers in the oceans of the world.

Directions: Read each sentence. Circle the word or words from the pair in parentheses ( ) that correctly complete each sentence.

1. Because the jellyfish don't have to hunt for their food, there (was, was not) no need for stingers.

2. The beautiful jellyfish don't (never, ever) seem to be too bothered by human visitors.

3. El Niño brought high temperatures to Palau in the late 1990s. Suddenly, there weren't (any, no) jellyfish in the lake.

4. Write a sentence using one of these negative words: **no**, **none**, **never**, **nothing**, **nobody**, **nowhere**, **no one**, or **not**.

   _____

   _____

5. Write a sentence using a double negative. Then, write your sentence correctly.

   _____

   _____

   _____

   _____

LANGUAGE ARTS

Skill 98: Synonyms and Antonyms

Words that mean the **same** thing, or nearly the same thing, are called **synonyms**.

Directions: Circle a synonym for the underlined word in each row below. Then, write another synonym from the Word Bank in the blank.

Wow, you're speedy!

You're rather swift yourself!

Word Bank		
depressed phony	daring easy	attractive escape

1. <u>sad</u>   accident   unhappy   _____

2. <u>simple</u>   plain   plan   _____

3. <u>artificial</u>   flavor   fake   _____

4. <u>bold</u>   brave   warrior   _____

5. <u>beautiful</u>   pretty   dress   _____

6. <u>exit</u>   walk   leave   _____

Antonyms are words that are opposites.

Directions: Use the Word Bank to find an antonym for the boldfaced word in each sentence. The first one is done for you.

Word Bank					
open	light	late	hard	slow	old
right	full	below	clean	early	neat

1. My car was **dirty**, but now it is _____ clean _____.

2. My sister keeps her room **messy**, but I keep mine _____.

3. The sign said, "**Closed**," but the door was _____.

4. Is the glass half **empty** or half _____?

5. I bought **new** shoes, but I like my _____ ones better.

6. Skating is **easy** for me but _____ for my brother.

7. The sky is **dark** at night and _____ during the day.

8. Frank is often **tardy**, but Alyssa is usually _____.

9. My friend says I am **wrong**, but I say I am _____.

10. Jason is a **fast** runner, but Adam is a _____ runner.

11. We were supposed to be **early**, but we were _____.

LANGUAGE ARTS

Homophones are words that sound alike but have different spellings and meanings. Here are some examples of homophones.

Examples: Did you **hear** that noise?   The party is **here**.

Connor **knew** it would rain today.   I like your **new** haircut.

There is only **one** pancake left.   I **won** the raffle!

Our family is very large.   Pick Sam up in an **hour**.

Your mom speaks Spanish.   **You're** my best friend.

Directions: Read each sentence below. If the word in **bold** type is used correctly, make a check mark (✓) on the line. If it is not used correctly, write its homophone on the line.

1. _____ Mei **new** the best way to get from Seattle, Washington, to Portland, Oregon.

2. _____ We **eight** pie for dessert.

3. _____ **You're** sister said that Minnesota has long winters.

4. _____ My **hair** needed to be brushed.

5. _____ **Hour** class is going on a field trip to Pike Place Market.

6. _____ Is **your** boat docked in Puget Sound?

7. _____ The **bare** ran through the forest.

8. _____ The **knew** Seattle Central Library is a beautiful glass and steel building located downtown.

Directions: Read each sentence below. If the word in **bold** type is used correctly, make a check mark (✓) on the line. If it is not used correctly, write its homophone on the line.

1. _____ **I** saw the fog in the distance.

2. _____ The baby **dear** followed their mother through the trees.

3. _____ The **made** worked at the hotel.

4. _____ His **pail** face told me he was sick.

5. _____ You **brake** to stop the car.

6. _____ My cat has a long **tale**.

7. _____ I was **horse** from cheering at the hockey game.

8. _____ The store had a **sail**.

9. _____ I saw **one** of my old teachers today.

10. _____ Cory ripped the **seem** of his jacket.

11. _____ Grandma addressed the letter **too** me.

12. _____ Can you **right** in cursive?

Multiple-meaning words are words that are spelled the same but have different meanings. Look at how a word is used in a sentence to figure out which meaning it has.

In the first sentence below, the word **fair** means a **carnival**. In the second sentence, it means **equal** or **just**.

Jonah rode on a Ferris wheel at the county **fair**.

It is not **fair** that I have to go to bed an hour earlier than Amanda.

Directions: The dictionary entry below shows two different meanings for the same word. Each meaning is a different part of speech. Use the dictionary entry to answer the questions below.

watch *noun* a small device that is worn on the wrist and used to keep time
verb to look at or follow with one's eyes

1. Mikayla's grandparents gave her a watch for her birthday. Which definition of **watch** is used in this sentence? _____
   a. the first definition   **b.** the second definition

2. Did you watch the movie you rented? Which definition of **watch** is used in this sentence? _____
   a. the first definition   **b.** the second definition

3. What part of speech is **watch** when it is used to mean **a device used to keep time**? _____
   a. a noun   **b.** a verb

Skill 100: Multiple-Meaning Words

Directions: Read each sentence below. Choose the definition that matches the way the word in **bold** type is used in the sentence. Write the letter of the definition on the line.

1. _____ If you don't hurry, you'll miss the **train**!
   a. to teach something by repeating it
   b. a line of cars that move together along a track

2. _____ Mark scored a **goal** in the second half of the game.
   a. something that people work hard to achieve
   b. a score in a game when a puck or ball is shot into a certain area

3. _____ Eloise is the **second** child in a family of four girls.
   a. number two; the one that comes after the first
   b. a moment in time; a small part of a minute

4. _____ We dropped pennies in the **well** and made a wish for each one.
   a. healthy; good
   b. a deep hole in the ground, used to get water or oil

5. _____ Gabrielle's piano teacher is **patient** when she makes mistakes.
   a. not easily irritated or annoyed
   b. someone who is getting medical treatment

LANGUAGE ARTS

Answer Key

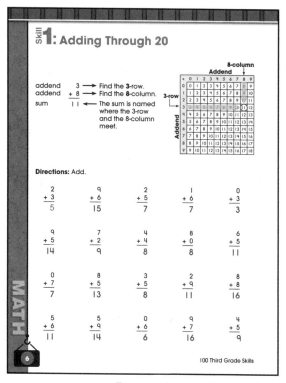

Skill 1: Adding Through 20

addend   3 → Find the **3**-row.
addend + 8 → Find the **8**-column.
sum   11 ← The sum is named where the 3-row and the 8-column meet.

Directions: Add.

$$\begin{array}{r} 2 \\ + 3 \\ \hline 5 \end{array} \quad \begin{array}{r} 9 \\ + 6 \\ \hline 15 \end{array} \quad \begin{array}{r} 2 \\ + 5 \\ \hline 7 \end{array} \quad \begin{array}{r} 1 \\ + 6 \\ \hline 7 \end{array} \quad \begin{array}{r} 0 \\ + 3 \\ \hline 3 \end{array}$$

$$\begin{array}{r} 9 \\ + 5 \\ \hline 14 \end{array} \quad \begin{array}{r} 7 \\ + 2 \\ \hline 9 \end{array} \quad \begin{array}{r} 4 \\ + 4 \\ \hline 8 \end{array} \quad \begin{array}{r} 8 \\ + 0 \\ \hline 8 \end{array} \quad \begin{array}{r} 6 \\ + 5 \\ \hline 11 \end{array}$$

$$\begin{array}{r} 0 \\ + 7 \\ \hline 7 \end{array} \quad \begin{array}{r} 8 \\ + 5 \\ \hline 13 \end{array} \quad \begin{array}{r} 3 \\ + 5 \\ \hline 8 \end{array} \quad \begin{array}{r} 2 \\ + 9 \\ \hline 11 \end{array} \quad \begin{array}{r} 8 \\ + 8 \\ \hline 16 \end{array}$$

$$\begin{array}{r} 5 \\ + 6 \\ \hline 11 \end{array} \quad \begin{array}{r} 5 \\ + 9 \\ \hline 14 \end{array} \quad \begin{array}{r} 0 \\ + 6 \\ \hline 6 \end{array} \quad \begin{array}{r} 9 \\ + 7 \\ \hline 16 \end{array} \quad \begin{array}{r} 4 \\ + 5 \\ \hline 9 \end{array}$$

MATH

6

100 Third Grade Skills

Page 6

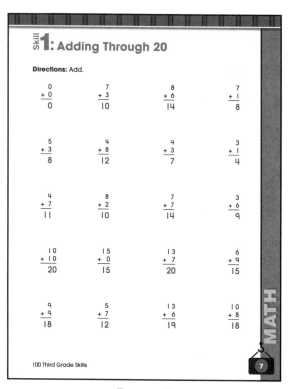

Skill 1: Adding Through 20

Directions: Add.

$$\begin{array}{r} 0 \\ + 0 \\ \hline 0 \end{array} \quad \begin{array}{r} 7 \\ + 3 \\ \hline 10 \end{array} \quad \begin{array}{r} 8 \\ + 6 \\ \hline 14 \end{array} \quad \begin{array}{r} 7 \\ + 1 \\ \hline 8 \end{array}$$

$$\begin{array}{r} 5 \\ + 3 \\ \hline 8 \end{array} \quad \begin{array}{r} 4 \\ + 8 \\ \hline 12 \end{array} \quad \begin{array}{r} 4 \\ + 3 \\ \hline 7 \end{array} \quad \begin{array}{r} 3 \\ + 1 \\ \hline 4 \end{array}$$

$$\begin{array}{r} 4 \\ + 7 \\ \hline 11 \end{array} \quad \begin{array}{r} 8 \\ + 2 \\ \hline 10 \end{array} \quad \begin{array}{r} 7 \\ + 7 \\ \hline 14 \end{array} \quad \begin{array}{r} 3 \\ + 6 \\ \hline 9 \end{array}$$

$$\begin{array}{r} 10 \\ + 10 \\ \hline 20 \end{array} \quad \begin{array}{r} 15 \\ + 0 \\ \hline 15 \end{array} \quad \begin{array}{r} 13 \\ + 7 \\ \hline 20 \end{array} \quad \begin{array}{r} 6 \\ + 9 \\ \hline 15 \end{array}$$

$$\begin{array}{r} 9 \\ + 9 \\ \hline 18 \end{array} \quad \begin{array}{r} 5 \\ + 7 \\ \hline 12 \end{array} \quad \begin{array}{r} 13 \\ + 6 \\ \hline 19 \end{array} \quad \begin{array}{r} 10 \\ + 8 \\ \hline 18 \end{array}$$

100 Third Grade Skills

MATH

7

Page 7

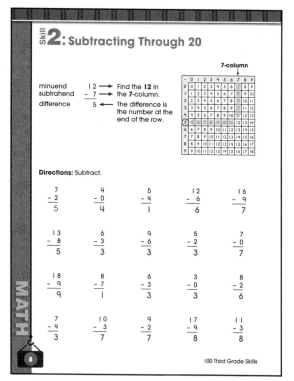

Skill 2: Subtracting Through 20

minuend   12 → Find the **12** in the **7**-column.
subtrahend – 7 →
difference   5 ← The difference is the number at the end of the row.

Directions: Subtract.

$$\begin{array}{r} 7 \\ - 2 \\ \hline 5 \end{array} \quad \begin{array}{r} 4 \\ - 0 \\ \hline 4 \end{array} \quad \begin{array}{r} 5 \\ - 4 \\ \hline 1 \end{array} \quad \begin{array}{r} 12 \\ - 6 \\ \hline 6 \end{array} \quad \begin{array}{r} 16 \\ - 9 \\ \hline 7 \end{array}$$

$$\begin{array}{r} 13 \\ - 8 \\ \hline 5 \end{array} \quad \begin{array}{r} 6 \\ - 3 \\ \hline 3 \end{array} \quad \begin{array}{r} 9 \\ - 6 \\ \hline 3 \end{array} \quad \begin{array}{r} 5 \\ - 2 \\ \hline 3 \end{array} \quad \begin{array}{r} 7 \\ - 0 \\ \hline 7 \end{array}$$

$$\begin{array}{r} 18 \\ - 9 \\ \hline 9 \end{array} \quad \begin{array}{r} 8 \\ - 7 \\ \hline 1 \end{array} \quad \begin{array}{r} 6 \\ - 3 \\ \hline 3 \end{array} \quad \begin{array}{r} 3 \\ - 0 \\ \hline 3 \end{array} \quad \begin{array}{r} 8 \\ - 2 \\ \hline 6 \end{array}$$

$$\begin{array}{r} 7 \\ - 4 \\ \hline 3 \end{array} \quad \begin{array}{r} 10 \\ - 3 \\ \hline 7 \end{array} \quad \begin{array}{r} 9 \\ - 2 \\ \hline 7 \end{array} \quad \begin{array}{r} 17 \\ - 9 \\ \hline 8 \end{array} \quad \begin{array}{r} 11 \\ - 3 \\ \hline 8 \end{array}$$

MATH

8

100 Third Grade Skills

Page 8

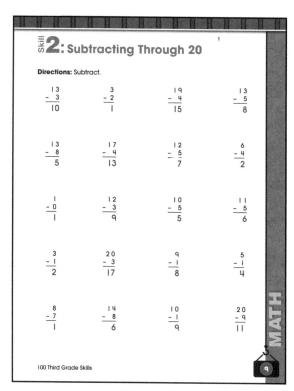

Skill 2: Subtracting Through 20

Directions: Subtract.

$$\begin{array}{r} 13 \\ - 3 \\ \hline 10 \end{array} \quad \begin{array}{r} 3 \\ - 2 \\ \hline 1 \end{array} \quad \begin{array}{r} 19 \\ - 4 \\ \hline 15 \end{array} \quad \begin{array}{r} 13 \\ - 5 \\ \hline 8 \end{array}$$

$$\begin{array}{r} 13 \\ - 8 \\ \hline 5 \end{array} \quad \begin{array}{r} 17 \\ - 4 \\ \hline 13 \end{array} \quad \begin{array}{r} 12 \\ - 5 \\ \hline 7 \end{array} \quad \begin{array}{r} 6 \\ - 4 \\ \hline 2 \end{array}$$

$$\begin{array}{r} 1 \\ - 0 \\ \hline 1 \end{array} \quad \begin{array}{r} 12 \\ - 3 \\ \hline 9 \end{array} \quad \begin{array}{r} 10 \\ - 5 \\ \hline 5 \end{array} \quad \begin{array}{r} 11 \\ - 5 \\ \hline 6 \end{array}$$

$$\begin{array}{r} 3 \\ - 1 \\ \hline 2 \end{array} \quad \begin{array}{r} 20 \\ - 3 \\ \hline 17 \end{array} \quad \begin{array}{r} 9 \\ - 1 \\ \hline 8 \end{array} \quad \begin{array}{r} 5 \\ - 1 \\ \hline 4 \end{array}$$

$$\begin{array}{r} 8 \\ - 7 \\ \hline 1 \end{array} \quad \begin{array}{r} 14 \\ - 8 \\ \hline 6 \end{array} \quad \begin{array}{r} 10 \\ - 1 \\ \hline 9 \end{array} \quad \begin{array}{r} 20 \\ - 9 \\ \hline 11 \end{array}$$

100 Third Grade Skills

MATH

9

Page 9

100 Third Grade Skills

Answer Key

Page 10

First, add the ones.   Then, add the tens.

$$\begin{array}{r} 4\,3 \\ +\,2\,2 \\ \hline 5 \end{array} \qquad \begin{array}{r} 4\,3 \\ +\,2\,2 \\ \hline \end{array} \qquad \begin{array}{r} 4\,3 \\ +\,2\,2 \\ \hline 6\,5 \end{array}$$

addend
addend
addend
sum

$$\begin{array}{r} 2\,2 \\ +\,1\,6 \\ \hline 3\,8 \end{array}$$

addend
addend
sum
First, add the ones.
Then, add the tens.

Directions: Add.

23 + 16 **39**	22 + 33 **55**	20 + 10 **30**	15 + 11 **26**	73 + 15 **88**
63 + 13 **76**	10 + 16 **26**	18 + 30 **48**	13 + 14 **27**	33 + 41 **74**
81 + 11 **92**	34 + 21 **55**	14 + 12 **26**	43 + 12 **55**	41 + 18 **59**
40 + 30 **70**	27 + 50 **77**	22 + 22 **44**	54 + 34 **88**	36 + 13 **49**

MATH
10
100 Third Grade Skills

Page 11

Directions: Add.

17 + 51 **68**	13 + 42 **55**	12 + 44 **56**	32 + 16 **48**
27 + 42 **69**	31 + 38 **69**	13 + 14 **27**	15 + 44 **59**
23 + 42 **65**	22 + 71 **93**	36 + 50 **86**	35 + 23 **58**
10 + 43 **53**	73 + 20 **93**	86 + 13 **99**	52 + 13 **65**
42 + 26 **68**	32 + 45 **77**	61 + 31 **92**	25 + 24 **49**

100 Third Grade Skills
MATH
11

Page 12

First, subtract the ones.   Then, subtract the tens.

$$\begin{array}{r} 3\,6 \\ -\,2\,3 \\ \hline 3 \end{array} \qquad \begin{array}{r} 3\,6 \\ -\,2\,3 \\ \hline \end{array} \qquad \begin{array}{r} 3\,6 \\ -\,2\,3 \\ \hline 1\,3 \end{array}$$

minuend
subtrahend
difference

Directions: Subtract.

23 − 12 **15**	76 − 22 **54**	93 − 71 **22**	30 − 10 **20**	92 − 11 **81**
48 − 16 **32**	62 − 10 **52**	83 − 13 **70**	65 − 44 **21**	33 − 12 **21**
37 − 25 **12**	88 − 32 **56**	86 − 45 **41**	82 − 70 **12**	89 − 62 **27**
75 − 62 **13**	77 − 44 **33**	90 − 60 **30**	74 − 22 **52**	96 − 53 **43**

MATH
12
100 Third Grade Skills

Page 13

Directions: Subtract.

82 − 41 **41**	47 − 36 **11**	35 − 23 **12**	66 − 43 **23**
81 − 60 **21**	42 − 30 **12**	50 − 30 **20**	46 − 25 **21**
92 − 81 **11**	75 − 32 **43**	57 − 36 **21**	29 − 13 **16**
25 − 15 **10**	28 − 12 **16**	46 − 13 **33**	46 − 15 **31**
75 − 14 **61**	64 − 23 **41**	59 − 45 **14**	83 − 11 **72**

100 Third Grade Skills
MATH
13

Answer Key

Skill 5: Adding 2-Digit Numbers (No Renaming)

Add the ones. Rename 12 as 10 + 2.   Add the tens.

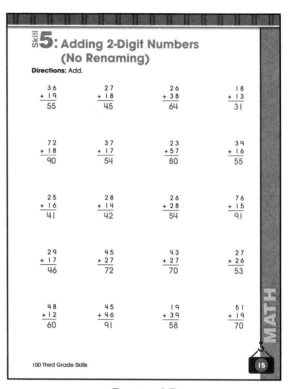

Directions: Add.

23 +18 **41**	76 +15 **91**	14 +77 **91**	36 +16 **52**	18 +62 **80**
29 +19 **48**	27 +36 **63**	42 +39 **81**	36 +28 **64**	17 +16 **33**
56 +27 **83**	59 +13 **72**	54 +27 **81**	33 +28 **61**	28 +17 **45**
13 +19 **32**	49 +17 **66**	56 +14 **70**	68 +23 **91**	37 +46 **83**

100 Third Grade Skills

14

Page 14

Skill 5: Adding 2-Digit Numbers (No Renaming)

Directions: Add.

36 +19 **55**	27 +18 **45**	26 +38 **64**	18 +13 **31**
72 +18 **90**	37 +17 **54**	23 +57 **80**	39 +16 **55**
25 +16 **41**	28 +14 **42**	26 +28 **54**	76 +15 **91**
29 +17 **46**	45 +27 **72**	43 +27 **70**	27 +26 **53**
48 +12 **60**	45 +46 **91**	19 +39 **58**	51 +19 **70**

100 Third Grade Skills

15

Page 15

Skill 6: Subtracting 2-Digit Numbers (No Renaming)

Subtract the ones. Rename 52 as "4 tens and 12 ones."   Subtract the ones.   Subtract the tens.

52 -19	5̸2̸ -19	5̸2̸ -19 3	5̸2̸ -19 33	minuend subtrahend difference

Directions: Subtract.

30 -22 **8**	22 -19 **3**	43 -28 **15**	41 -27 **14**	82 -56 **26**
86 -27 **59**	83 -66 **17**	61 -56 **5**	51 -17 **34**	33 -15 **18**
46 -29 **17**	57 -38 **19**	72 -37 **35**	72 -67 **5**	64 -18 **46**
76 -57 **19**	41 -16 **25**	53 -29 **24**	65 -46 **19**	97 -79 **8**

100 Third Grade Skills

16

Page 16

Skill 6: Subtracting 2-Digit Numbers (No Renaming)

Directions: Subtract.

24 -17 **7**	50 -20 **30**	86 -27 **59**	83 -26 **57**
52 -17 **35**	47 -28 **19**	86 -38 **48**	45 -18 **27**
41 -19 **22**	96 -39 **57**	63 -27 **36**	87 -68 **19**
53 -17 **36**	92 -45 **47**	86 -18 **68**	72 -17 **55**
63 -45 **18**	52 -13 **39**	81 -48 **33**	34 -26 **8**

100 Third Grade Skills

17

Page 17

Answer Key

Skill 7: Adding Three Numbers

Add the ones.

```
2 3    3⌐
4 7    7 ⟩ 10
+1 6   6⌐
              16 or 10 + 6
```

```
2 3
4 7
+1 6
    6
```

Add the tens.

```
  1
2 3   addend
4 7   addend
+1 6  addend
8 6   sum
```

Directions: Add.

```
 1 3      6      1 6     2 8      6
 2 6     2 9     2 3      7      1 3
+4 5    +4 3    +2 5    +3 3    +2 9
 8 4     7 8     6 4     6 8     4 8
```

```
 1 0     2 2     1 8     2 9     1 3
 3 0     3 1     2 1     1 6     1 5
+5 0    +4 5    +3 3    +1 5    +2 5
 9 0     9 8     7 2     6 0     5 3
```

```
 4 1     2 6     1 1     2 7      4
 2 1     2 3     3 0     1 6      7
+ 8    +3 5    +4 2    + 8    + 8
 7 0     8 4     8 3     5 1     1 9
```

100 Third Grade Skills

18

Page 18

Skill 7: Adding Three Numbers

Directions: Add.

```
 3 4     1 6     2 9     8 1
 1 6     2 3     3 1      5
+4 1    +3 5    +2 5    + 6
 9 1     7 4     8 5     9 2
```

```
 3 3     7 6     1 8     4 1
 4 7      5     3 2     2 9
+1 2    + 3    +1 6    +1 6
 9 2     8 4     6 6     8 6
```

```
 5 3     6 6     4 7     2 2
 2 1     2 1     1 4     4 1
+1 5    + 8    + 8    +2 8
 8 9     9 5     6 9     9 1
```

```
 2 3     1 8     2 3     6 4
 1 3     1 6     3 5     2 7
+1 7    +2 4    +1 7    + 4
 5 3     5 8     7 5     9 5
```

100 Third Grade Skills

19

Page 19

Skill 8: Subtracting 2 Digits From 3 Digits

Subtract the ones.

```
1 2 5
- 8 4
```

To subtract the tens, rename the 1 hundred and 2 tens as "12 tens."

```
1 2 5
- 8 4
    1
```

```
  12
1 2̸ 5
- 8 4
    1
```

Subtract the tens.

```
   12
1 2̸ 5   minuend
- 8 4    subtrahend
  4 1    difference
```

Directions: Subtract.

```
1 7 3    1 2 1    1 9 5    1 2 2    1 4 7
- 3 3    - 6 0    - 4 4    - 1 1    - 5 3
1 4 0     6 1     1 5 1    1 1 1     9 4
```

```
1 8 2    1 4 3    1 8 0    1 1 9    1 2 3
- 9 0    - 6 2    - 7 0    - 1 5    - 1 2
  9 2     8 1     1 1 0    1 0 4    1 1 1
```

```
1 8 6    1 8 7    1 5 4    1 2 7    1 8 7
- 6 5    - 4 2    - 1 3    - 8 3    - 6 7
1 2 1    1 4 5    1 4 1     4 4     1 2 0
```

```
1 3 5    1 1 5    1 7 1    1 4 8    1 9 1
- 4 2    - 2 4    - 6 0    - 5 6    - 7 7
  9 3     9 1     1 1 1     9 2     1 1 4
```

100 Third Grade Skills

20

Page 20

Skill 8: Subtracting 2 Digits From 3 Digits

Directions: Subtract.

```
1 3 2    1 7 7    1 9 2    1 8 6
- 5 1    - 4 3    - 7 1    - 9 2
  8 1     1 3 4   1 2 1     9 4
```

```
1 3 4    1 2 5    1 2 9    1 7 6
- 7 2    - 4 5    - 8 6    - 7 5
  6 2     8 0      4 3     1 0 1
```

```
1 2 0    1 9 4    1 8 9    1 3 4
- 4 0    - 5 3    - 6 2    - 4 2
  8 0     1 4 1   1 2 7     9 2
```

```
1 6 5    1 6 7    1 5 0    1 5 7
- 5 1    - 4 5    - 3 0    - 6 3
1 1 4    1 2 2    1 2 0     9 4
```

```
1 4 9    1 3 9    1 7 5    1 6 7
- 6 1    - 6 2    - 8 2    - 4 3
  8 8     7 7      9 3     1 2 4
```

```
1 3 3    1 4 8    1 6 5    1 2 8
- 4 1    - 7 8    - 4 3    - 5 7
  9 2     7 0     1 2 2     7 1
```

100 Third Grade Skills

21

Page 21

Answer Key

Page 22

Skill 9: Adding 3-Digit Numbers

Add the ones.	Add the tens.	Add the hundreds.

$$755 + 469$$

$$\begin{array}{r} 755 \\ +469 \\ \hline 4 \end{array} \quad \begin{array}{r} 755 \\ +469 \\ \hline 24 \end{array} \quad \begin{array}{r} 755 \\ +469 \\ \hline 1224 \end{array}$$

Directions: Add.

123 +562 = 685	982 +171 = 1,153	342 +591 = 933	782 +341 = 1,123	123 +321 = 444
681 +975 = 1,656	862 +313 = 1,175	900 +130 = 1,030	720 +850 = 1,570	931 +111 = 1,042
823 +457 = 1,280	547 +321 = 868	861 +421 = 1,282	862 +139 = 1,001	431 +250 = 681
782 +191 = 973	751 +605 = 1,356	871 +323 = 1,194	337 +488 = 825	606 +222 = 828

MATH

22

100 Third Grade Skills

Page 23

Skill 9: Adding 3-Digit Numbers

Directions: Add.

791 +191 = 982	144 +800 = 944	192 +175 = 367	257 +147 = 404
203 +211 = 414	541 +693 = 1,234	705 +719 = 1,424	641 +209 = 850
873 +505 = 1,378	700 +650 = 1,350	105 +341 = 446	450 +362 = 812
593 +741 = 1,334	861 +209 = 1,070	735 +145 = 880	820 +431 = 1,251
738 +387 = 1,125	719 +120 = 839	153 +312 = 465	712 +210 = 922
619 +715 = 1,334	205 +316 = 521	153 +814 = 967	613 +261 = 874

100 Third Grade Skills

MATH

23

Page 24

Skill 10: Subtracting 3-Digit Numbers

Rename 2 tens and 1 one as "1 ten and 11 ones." Then, subtract the ones.	Rename 6 hundreds and 1 ten as "5 hundreds and 11 tens." Then, subtract the tens.	Subtract the hundreds.

$$\begin{array}{r} 621 \\ -259 \\ \hline \end{array} \quad \begin{array}{r} 6\overset{1\,11}{\cancel{2}\cancel{1}} \\ -259 \\ \hline 2 \end{array} \quad \begin{array}{r} \overset{5}{\cancel{6}}\overset{11}{\cancel{2}}\cancel{1} \\ -259 \\ \hline 62 \end{array} \quad \begin{array}{r} \overset{5}{\cancel{6}}\overset{11}{\cancel{2}}\cancel{1} \\ -259 \\ \hline 362 \end{array}$$

minuend
subtrahend
difference

Directions: Subtract.

321 -109 = 212	745 -152 = 593	639 -150 = 489	830 -710 = 120	626 -146 = 480
457 -309 = 148	729 -321 = 408	657 -451 = 206	386 -107 = 279	411 -305 = 106
486 -109 = 377	311 -121 = 190	983 -652 = 331	971 -572 = 399	876 -357 = 519
549 -360 = 189	721 -144 = 577	958 -637 = 321	644 -428 = 216	909 -875 = 34

MATH

24

100 Third Grade Skills

Page 25

Skill 10: Subtracting 3-Digit Numbers

Directions: Subtract.

256 -142 = 114	347 -139 = 208	725 -196 = 529	863 -692 = 171
980 -532 = 448	720 -500 = 220	543 -457 = 86	762 -135 = 627
132 -107 = 25	921 -571 = 350	631 -545 = 86	982 -144 = 838
531 -250 = 281	720 -371 = 349	582 -357 = 225	793 -457 = 336
612 -483 = 129	592 -107 = 485	343 -240 = 103	916 -532 = 384

100 Third Grade Skills

MATH

25

100 Third Grade Skills

Answer Key

Page 26

Skill 11: Thinking Subtraction for Addition

To check
215 + 109 = 324,
subtract 109 from 324.

$$\begin{array}{r} 215 \\ +\ 109 \\ \hline 324 \\ -\ 109 \\ \hline 215 \end{array}$$
These should be the same.

Directions: Add. Check each answer.

$$\begin{array}{r} 157 \\ +212 \\ \hline 369 \\ -212 \\ \hline 157 \end{array} \qquad \begin{array}{r} 719 \\ +182 \\ \hline 901 \\ -182 \\ \hline 719 \end{array} \qquad \begin{array}{r} 312 \\ +105 \\ \hline 417 \\ -105 \\ \hline 312 \end{array} \qquad \begin{array}{r} 313 \\ +619 \\ \hline 932 \\ -619 \\ \hline 313 \end{array}$$

$$\begin{array}{r} 306 \\ +215 \\ \hline 521 \\ -215 \\ \hline 306 \end{array} \qquad \begin{array}{r} 120 \\ +170 \\ \hline 290 \\ -170 \\ \hline 120 \end{array} \qquad \begin{array}{r} 710 \\ +398 \\ \hline 1,108 \\ -398 \\ \hline 710 \end{array} \qquad \begin{array}{r} 457 \\ +349 \\ \hline 806 \\ -349 \\ \hline 457 \end{array}$$

$$\begin{array}{r} 712 \\ +363 \\ \hline 1,075 \\ -363 \\ \hline 712 \end{array} \qquad \begin{array}{r} 714 \\ +291 \\ \hline 1,005 \\ -291 \\ \hline 714 \end{array} \qquad \begin{array}{r} 311 \\ +\ 88 \\ \hline 399 \\ -\ 88 \\ \hline 311 \end{array} \qquad \begin{array}{r} 419 \\ +\ 57 \\ \hline 476 \\ -\ 57 \\ \hline 419 \end{array}$$

26
100 Third Grade Skills

Page 27

Skill 11: Thinking Subtraction for Addition

Directions: Add. Check each answer.

$$\begin{array}{r} 400 \\ +547 \\ \hline 947 \\ -547 \\ \hline 400 \end{array} \qquad \begin{array}{r} 591 \\ +120 \\ \hline 711 \\ -120 \\ \hline 591 \end{array} \qquad \begin{array}{r} 612 \\ +319 \\ \hline 931 \\ -319 \\ \hline 612 \end{array} \qquad \begin{array}{r} 325 \\ +125 \\ \hline 450 \\ -125 \\ \hline 325 \end{array}$$

$$\begin{array}{r} 411 \\ +120 \\ \hline 531 \\ -120 \\ \hline 411 \end{array} \qquad \begin{array}{r} 247 \\ +259 \\ \hline 506 \\ -259 \\ \hline 247 \end{array} \qquad \begin{array}{r} 863 \\ +192 \\ \hline 1,055 \\ -\ 192 \\ \hline 863 \end{array} \qquad \begin{array}{r} 459 \\ +130 \\ \hline 589 \\ -130 \\ \hline 459 \end{array}$$

$$\begin{array}{r} 303 \\ +209 \\ \hline 512 \\ -209 \\ \hline 303 \end{array} \qquad \begin{array}{r} 711 \\ +191 \\ \hline 902 \\ -191 \\ \hline 711 \end{array} \qquad \begin{array}{r} 252 \\ +130 \\ \hline 382 \\ -130 \\ \hline 252 \end{array} \qquad \begin{array}{r} 411 \\ +283 \\ \hline 694 \\ -283 \\ \hline 411 \end{array}$$

$$\begin{array}{r} 601 \\ +176 \\ \hline 777 \\ -176 \\ \hline 601 \end{array} \qquad \begin{array}{r} 575 \\ +251 \\ \hline 826 \\ -251 \\ \hline 575 \end{array} \qquad \begin{array}{r} 723 \\ +197 \\ \hline 920 \\ -197 \\ \hline 723 \end{array} \qquad \begin{array}{r} 358 \\ +492 \\ \hline 850 \\ -492 \\ \hline 358 \end{array}$$

100 Third Grade Skills
27

Page 28

Skill 12: Thinking Addition for Subtraction

To check
982 − 657 = 325,
add 657 to 325.

$$\begin{array}{r} 982 \\ -\ 657 \\ \hline 325 \\ +\ 657 \\ \hline 982 \end{array}$$
These should be the same.

Directions: Subtract. Check each answer.

$$\begin{array}{r} 720 \\ -150 \\ \hline 570 \\ +150 \\ \hline 720 \end{array} \qquad \begin{array}{r} 321 \\ -\ 83 \\ \hline 238 \\ +\ 83 \\ \hline 321 \end{array} \qquad \begin{array}{r} 126 \\ -\ 92 \\ \hline 34 \\ +\ 92 \\ \hline 126 \end{array} \qquad \begin{array}{r} 983 \\ -657 \\ \hline 326 \\ +657 \\ \hline 983 \end{array}$$

$$\begin{array}{r} 456 \\ -291 \\ \hline 165 \\ +291 \\ \hline 456 \end{array} \qquad \begin{array}{r} 442 \\ -220 \\ \hline 222 \\ +220 \\ \hline 442 \end{array} \qquad \begin{array}{r} 300 \\ -179 \\ \hline 121 \\ +179 \\ \hline 300 \end{array} \qquad \begin{array}{r} 117 \\ -104 \\ \hline 13 \\ +104 \\ \hline 117 \end{array}$$

$$\begin{array}{r} 423 \\ -197 \\ \hline 226 \\ +197 \\ \hline 423 \end{array} \qquad \begin{array}{r} 259 \\ -147 \\ \hline 112 \\ +147 \\ \hline 259 \end{array} \qquad \begin{array}{r} 638 \\ -463 \\ \hline 175 \\ +463 \\ \hline 638 \end{array} \qquad \begin{array}{r} 708 \\ -412 \\ \hline 296 \\ +412 \\ \hline 708 \end{array}$$

28
100 Third Grade Skills

Page 29

Skill 12: Thinking Addition for Subtraction

Directions: Subtract. Check each answer.

$$\begin{array}{r} 519 \\ -120 \\ \hline 399 \\ +120 \\ \hline 519 \end{array} \qquad \begin{array}{r} 640 \\ -320 \\ \hline 320 \\ +320 \\ \hline 640 \end{array} \qquad \begin{array}{r} 192 \\ -\ 86 \\ \hline 106 \\ +\ 86 \\ \hline 192 \end{array} \qquad \begin{array}{r} 710 \\ -441 \\ \hline 269 \\ +441 \\ \hline 710 \end{array}$$

$$\begin{array}{r} 683 \\ -419 \\ \hline 264 \\ +419 \\ \hline 683 \end{array} \qquad \begin{array}{r} 712 \\ -307 \\ \hline 405 \\ +307 \\ \hline 712 \end{array} \qquad \begin{array}{r} 719 \\ -532 \\ \hline 187 \\ +532 \\ \hline 719 \end{array} \qquad \begin{array}{r} 919 \\ -457 \\ \hline 462 \\ +457 \\ \hline 919 \end{array}$$

$$\begin{array}{r} 731 \\ -250 \\ \hline 481 \\ +250 \\ \hline 731 \end{array} \qquad \begin{array}{r} 912 \\ -609 \\ \hline 303 \\ +609 \\ \hline 912 \end{array} \qquad \begin{array}{r} 542 \\ -327 \\ \hline 215 \\ +327 \\ \hline 542 \end{array} \qquad \begin{array}{r} 728 \\ -530 \\ \hline 198 \\ +530 \\ \hline 728 \end{array}$$

$$\begin{array}{r} 939 \\ -482 \\ \hline 457 \\ -482 \\ \hline 939 \end{array} \qquad \begin{array}{r} 766 \\ -149 \\ \hline 617 \\ -149 \\ \hline 766 \end{array} \qquad \begin{array}{r} 819 \\ -640 \\ \hline 179 \\ -640 \\ \hline 819 \end{array} \qquad \begin{array}{r} 643 \\ -391 \\ \hline 252 \\ -391 \\ \hline 643 \end{array}$$

100 Third Grade Skills
29

Answer Key

Page 30

Skill 13: Adding 3 or More Numbers
(1- and 2-digit)

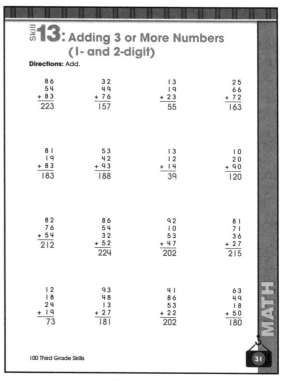

Add the ones.

```
  45        5  →1        45         1
  62        2 →7         62        45
+ 94       +4  +4       +94        62
                   11 or 10 + 1          +94
                                   Add the tens.
                                   45
                                   62
                                  +94
                                  201
```

Directions: Add.

```
   3      7      6      8     12
   6      5     12     17     32
 + 9    + 8   + 13   + 19   + 53
  18     20     31     44     97
```

```
   8     17     16     82      7
   6     93     45     18     19
 + 2   + 23   + 92   + 23   + 57
  16    133    153    123     83
```

```
  22     50     86     23     18
  86     40     93     35     35
+ 34   + 60   + 72   + 62   + 67
 142    150    251    120    120
```

100 Third Grade Skills

30

Page 31

Skill 13: Adding 3 or More Numbers
(1- and 2-digit)

Directions: Add.

```
  86     32     13     25
  54     49     19     66
+ 83   + 76   + 23   + 72
 223    157     55    163
```

```
  81     53     13     10
  19     42     12     20
+ 83   + 93   + 14   + 90
 183    188     39    120
```

```
  82     86     92     81
  76     54     10     71
+ 54     32     53     36
 212   + 52   + 47   + 27
        224    202    215
```

```
  12     93     41     63
  18     48     86     49
  24     13     53     18
+ 19   + 27   + 22   + 50
  73    181    202    180
```

100 Third Grade Skills

31

Page 32

Skill 14: Adding 3 or More Numbers
(3-digit)

```
Add the ones.   Add the tens.   Add the hundreds.
    1              11              11
  231    231      231      231
  457    457      457      457
+ 625  + 625    + 625    + 625
            3       13     1313
```

Directions: Add.

```
 522    868    150    701    986
 367    321    200    231    105
+ 151  + 405  + 300  + 862  + 525
1,040  1,594    650  1,794  1,616
```

```
 129    803    545    868    132
 318    623    309    740    195
+ 467  + 186  + 119  + 809  + 118
 914   1,612    973  2,417    445
```

```
 200    180    861    863    731
 300    240    757    404    356
+ 600  + 303  + 409  + 891  + 402
1,100    723  2,027  2,158  1,489
```

100 Third Grade Skills

32

Page 33

Skill 14: Adding 3 or More Numbers
(3-digit)

Directions: Add.

```
 865    238    898    341
 591    405    777    127
+ 217  + 596  + 192  + 192
1,673  1,239  1,867    660
```

```
 864    127    205    712
 425    291    876    490
+ 323  + 867  + 198  + 600
1,612  1,285  1,279  1,802
```

```
 750    591    862    892
 400    603    191    645
+ 203    907    183    320
1,353  + 432  + 251  + 123
       2,533  1,487  1,980
```

```
 132    323    712    212
 169    309    613    841
 119    452    518    360
+ 105  + 690  + 437  + 174
  525  1,774  2,280  1,587
```

100 Third Grade Skills

33

Answer Key

Skill 15: Adding 4-Digit Numbers

Add the ones.	Add the tens.	Add the hundreds.	Add the thousands.

```
  3746      3746      3746      3746       3746
+ 5899    + 5899    + 5899    + 5899     + 5899
              5        45       645        9645
```

Directions: Add.

```
  7865      8654      4320      3543      4293
+ 1192    + 1219    + 3069    + 3921    + 5176
  9,057     9,873     7,389     7,464     9,469

  6405      1982      7083      4325      6057
+ 3398    + 1782    + 2907    + 4986    + 1239
  9,803     3,764     9,990     9,311     7,296

  8761      2305      3050      6932      5437
+ 1032    + 5747    + 4707    + 2349    + 2968
  9,793     8,052     7,757     9,281     8,405

  1718      7923      4523      5111      3597
+ 2347    + 1250    + 3962    + 2699    + 4922
  4,065     9,173     8,485     7,810     8,519
```

Page 34

Skill 15: Adding 4-Digit Numbers

Directions: Add.

```
  5431      7986      1119      7239
+ 2989    + 1479    + 2459    + 1635
  8,420     9,465     3,578     8,874

  2450      6527      5431      7986
+ 7267    + 2985    + 1982    + 1246
  9,717     9,512     7,413     9,232

  1543      7121      8763      4321
+ 3989    + 1923    + 1005    + 2387
  5,532     9,044     9,768     6,708

  5450      4733      3981      6986
+ 1987    + 2576    + 2877    + 2928
  7,437     7,309     6,858     9,914

  7181      7900      6919      2873
+ 2111    + 2005    + 1255    + 5464
  9,292     9,905     8,174     8,337
```

Page 35

Skill 16: Subtracting to 4 Digits

Subtract the ones.	Rename 4 hundreds and 3 tens as "3 hundreds and 13 tens." Subtract the tens.	Rename 5 thousands and 3 hundreds as "4 thousands and 13 hundreds." Subtract the hundreds.	Subtract the thousands.

```
  5437      5437      5437      5437       5437
- 1592    - 1592    - 1592    - 1592     - 1592
              5        45       845        3845
```

Directions: Subtract.

```
  9865      7528      8654      1925
- 2382    -  792    - 3993    -  183
  7,483     6,736     4,661     1,742

  1876      5473      8762      7945
-  982    - 3591    -  682    -  963
   894      1,882     8,080     6,982

  8654      7846      6932      1389
-  772    - 3974    - 2840    -  794
  7,882     3,872     4,092      595

  2545      7863      8121      9043
-  963    - 2572    -  640    - 2177
  1,582     5,291     7,481     6,866
```

Page 36

Skill 16: Subtracting to 4 Digits

Directions: Subtract.

```
  7865      3456      7982
-  974    -  661    -  490
  6,891     2,795     7,492

  8163      4325      9876
- 4670    - 1534    -  985
  3,493     2,791     8,891

  8716      5432      3287
- 5823    - 3651    -  395
  2,893     1,781     2,892

  7805      5439      4321
-  164    -  767    -  841
  7,641     4,672     3,480

  7865      7976      5439
-  974    - 4682    -  866
  6,891     3,294     4,573
```

Page 37

Answer Key

Skill 17: Rounding

Rounding numbers is a way of replacing one number with another number that tells about how many or how much.

When rounding to the nearest number, look at the digit to the right of it. If that column has 0, 1, 2, 3, or 4 in it, round down. If the column has 5, 6, 7, 8, or 9 in it, round up.

Round 23 to the nearest ten.
Look at the ones digit.

20   **23**   30

Round 23 down to 20.

Round 284 to the nearest hundred.
Look at the tens digit.

200   **284**   300

Round 284 up to 300.

Directions: Round the numbers to the place value listed.

	ten		hundred
23	20	483	500
567	570	809	800
775	780	495	500
2,813	2,810	311	300
408	410	407	400
742	740	3,054	3,100
384	380	609	600
99	100	937	900
826	830	148	100

38

100 Third Grade Skills

Page 38

Skill 17: Rounding

Directions: Draw an arrow to show which way to round the number to the nearest ten or hundred. Then, write the rounded number. The first one is done for you.

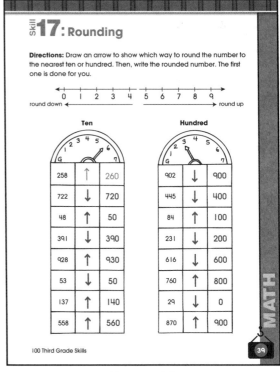

	Ten			Hundred	
258	↑	260	902	↓	900
722	↓	720	445	↓	400
48	↑	50	84	↑	100
391	↓	390	231	↓	200
928	↑	930	616	↓	600
53	↓	50	760	↑	800
137	↑	140	29	↓	0
558	↑	560	870	↑	900

100 Third Grade Skills

39

Page 39

Skill 18: Estimating Addition

Round each number to the highest place value the numbers have in common. Then, add from right to left.

$$\begin{array}{r} 194 \\ + \ 76 \end{array} \longrightarrow \begin{array}{r} 190 \\ + \ 80 \\ \hline 270 \end{array}$$

The highest place value for 194 and 76 is the tens place. Round 194 and 76 to the tens place. Add.

$$\begin{array}{r} 203 \\ + 196 \end{array} \longrightarrow \begin{array}{r} 200 \\ + 200 \\ \hline 400 \end{array}$$

The highest place value for 203 and 196 is the hundreds place. Round 203 and 196 to the hundreds place. Add.

Directions: Estimate each sum.

25 +36	30 +40 = 70	23 +14	20 +10 = 30	57 +51	60 +50 = 110		
42 +92	40 +90 = 130	92 +51	90 +50 = 140	131 +42	130 +40 = 170		
165 +92	170 +90 = 260	147 +97	150 +100 = 250	147 +362	100 +400 = 500		

40

100 Third Grade Skills

Page 40

Skill 18: Estimating Addition

Directions: Estimate each sum.

175 +302	200 +300 = 500	457 +603	500 +600 = 1,100	543 +261	500 +300 = 800
1132 +432	1100 +400 = 1,500	1250 +347	1300 +300 = 1,600	5786 +432	5800 +400 = 6,200
4679 +578	4700 +600 = 5,300	1562 +3492	2000 +3000 = 5,000	6054 +6542	6000 +7000 = 13,000
3541 +7987	4000 +8000 = 12,000	2795 +2454	3000 +2000 = 5,000	5232 +651	5200 +700 = 5,900

100 Third Grade Skills

41

Page 41

Answer Key

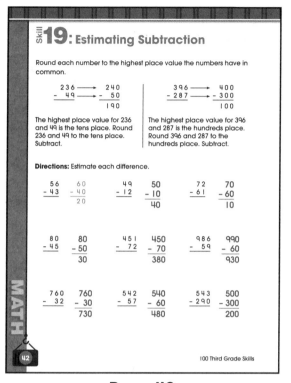

Page 42

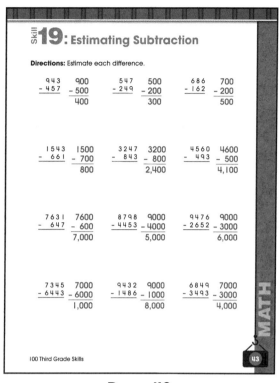

Page 43

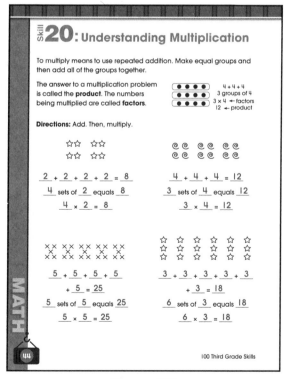

Page 44

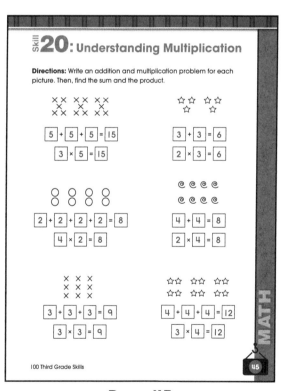

Page 45

Answer Key

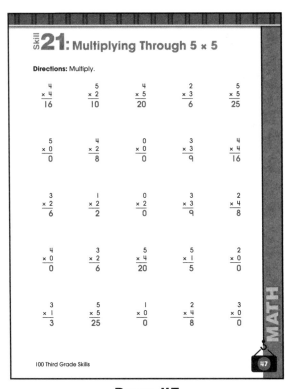

Skill 21: Multiplying Through 5 × 5

factor 3 → Find the 3-row.
factor × 5 → Find the 5-column.
product 1 5 ← The product is named where the 3-row and the 5-column meet.

Directions: Multiply.

| 2
× 5
10 | 5
× 3
15 | 1
× 3
3 | 1
× 4
4 |

| 3
× 4
12 | 5
× 2
10 | 0
× 5
0 | 1
× 1
1 |

| 3
× 5
15 | 2
× 2
4 | 0
× 3
0 | 4
× 3
12 |

46

100 Third Grade Skills

Page 46

Skill 21: Multiplying Through 5 × 5

Directions: Multiply.

| 4
× 4
16 | 5
× 2
10 | 4
× 5
20 | 2
× 3
6 | 5
× 5
25 |

| 5
× 0
0 | 4
× 2
8 | 0
× 0
0 | 3
× 3
9 | 4
× 4
16 |

| 3
× 2
6 | 1
× 2
2 | 0
× 2
0 | 3
× 3
9 | 2
× 4
8 |

| 4
× 0
0 | 3
× 2
6 | 5
× 4
20 | 5
× 1
5 | 2
× 0
0 |

| 3
× 1
3 | 5
× 5
25 | 1
× 0
0 | 2
× 4
8 | 3
× 0
0 |

100 Third Grade Skills

47

Page 47

Skill 22: Multiplying Through 5 × 9

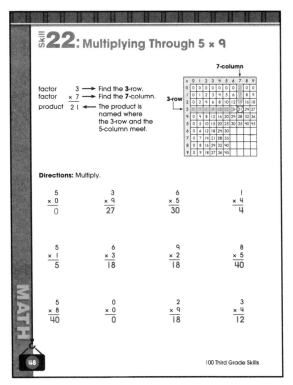

factor 3 → Find the 3-row.
factor × 7 → Find the 7-column.
product 2 1 ← The product is named where the 3-row and the 5-column meet.

Directions: Multiply.

| 5
× 0
0 | 3
× 9
27 | 6
× 5
30 | 1
× 4
4 |

| 5
× 1
5 | 6
× 3
18 | 9
× 2
18 | 8
× 5
40 |

| 5
× 8
40 | 0
× 0
0 | 2
× 9
18 | 3
× 4
12 |

48

100 Third Grade Skills

Page 48

Skill 22: Multiplying Through 5 × 9

Directions: Multiply.

| 4
× 6
24 | 7
× 3
21 | 6
× 1
6 | 7
× 2
14 | 3
× 5
15 |

| 4
× 1
4 | 6
× 2
12 | 5
× 5
25 | 9
× 1
9 | 2
× 4
8 |

| 3
× 7
21 | 7
× 0
0 | 0
× 9
0 | 3
× 6
18 | 7
× 5
35 |

| 5
× 6
30 | 3
× 2
6 | 4
× 2
8 | 7
× 4
28 | 3
× 3
9 |

| 1
× 9
9 | 2
× 7
14 | 0
× 6
0 | 1
× 3
3 | 4
× 5
20 |

100 Third Grade Skills

49

Page 49

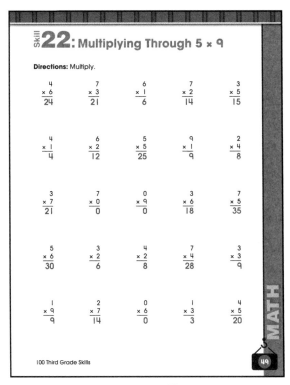

Answer Key

100 Third Grade Skills

Skill 23: Multiplying Through 9 × 9

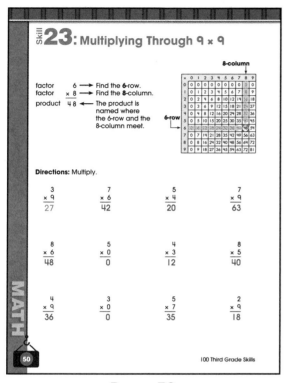

factor   6 ⟶ Find the **6**-row.
factor   × 8 ⟶ Find the **8**-column.
product   4 8 ⟵ The product is named where the 6-row and the 8-column meet.

Directions: Multiply.

| 3
× 9
27 | 7
× 6
42 | 5
× 4
20 | 7
× 9
63 |

| 8
× 6
48 | 5
× 0
0 | 4
× 3
12 | 8
× 5
40 |

| 4
× 9
36 | 3
× 0
0 | 5
× 7
35 | 2
× 9
18 |

50

100 Third Grade Skills

Page 50

Skill 23: Multiplying Through 9 × 9

Directions: Multiply.

| 5
× 1
5 | 4
× 6
24 | 8
× 2
16 | 6
× 8
48 | 4
× 0
0 |

| 0
× 9
0 | 3
× 1
3 | 6
× 4
24 | 9
× 2
18 | 3
× 4
12 |

| 6
× 3
18 | 5
× 6
30 | 3
× 8
24 | 3
× 6
18 | 7
× 6
42 |

| 9
× 9
81 | 8
× 4
32 | 5
× 3
15 | 2
× 6
12 | 8
× 8
64 |

| 9
× 3
27 | 7
× 4
28 | 8
× 0
0 | 7
× 7
49 | 9
× 8
72 |

100 Third Grade Skills

51

Page 51

Skill 24: Multiplying by Multiples of 10

Multiply 0 ones by 4.

| 70
× 4 | 70
× 4
0 | 70
× 4
280 |

Multiply 7 tens by 4.

Directions: Multiply.

| 30
× 3
90 | 20
× 1
20 | 10
× 9
90 | 60
× 4
240 | 80
× 2
160 |

| 70
× 7
490 | 40
× 5
200 | 50
× 8
400 | 90
× 6
540 | 40
× 2
80 |

| 80
× 5
400 | 60
× 8
480 | 90
× 2
180 | 10
× 5
50 | 20
× 7
140 |

| 50
× 3
150 | 70
× 3
210 | 30
× 5
150 | 20
× 4
80 | 10
× 3
30 |

52

100 Third Grade Skills

Page 52

Skill 24: Multiplying by Multiples of 10

Directions: Multiply.

| 90
× 4
360 | 70
× 9
630 | 60
× 2
120 | 50
× 5
250 | 20
× 5
100 |

| 50
× 3
150 | 10
× 3
30 | 10
× 4
40 | 30
× 4
120 | 50
× 2
100 |

| 30
× 5
150 | 10
× 4
40 | 30
× 6
180 | 20
× 2
40 | 70
× 3
210 |

| 40
× 3
120 | 40
× 4
160 | 80
× 2
160 | 40
× 6
240 | 20
× 7
140 |

| 50
× 6
300 | 50
× 5
250 | 40
× 8
320 | 90
× 0
0 | 70
× 5
350 |

| 40
× 9
360 | 30
× 2
60 | 10
× 8
80 | 60
× 5
300 | 80
× 8
640 |

100 Third Grade Skills

53

Page 53

Answer Key

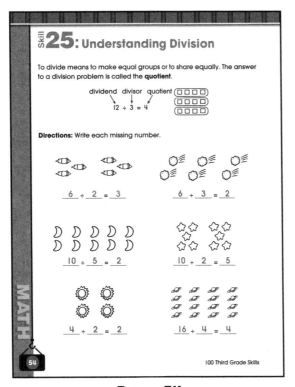

Page 54

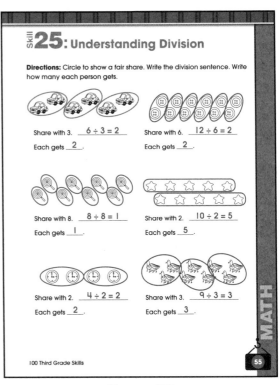

Page 55

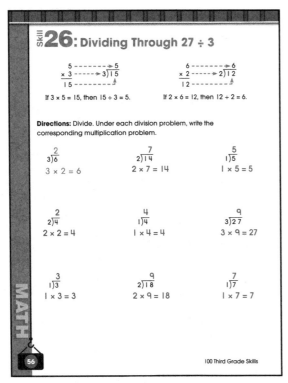

Page 56

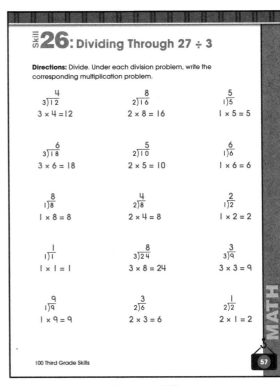

Page 57

Answer Key

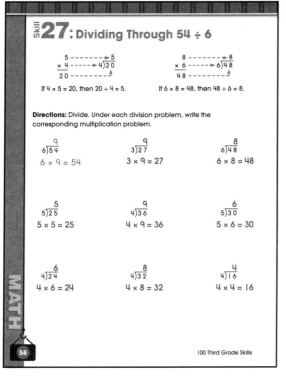

Page 58

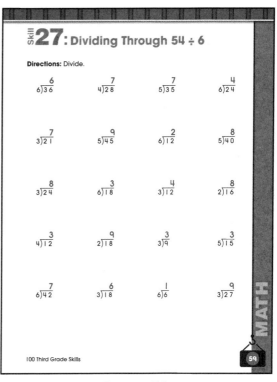

Page 59

Skill 28: Dividing Through 81 ÷ 9

$$\begin{array}{c} 6 \\ \times\,9 \\ \hline 54 \end{array} \longrightarrow \begin{array}{c} 6 \\ 9\overline{)54} \end{array} \qquad \begin{array}{c} 9 \\ \times\,7 \\ \hline 63 \end{array} \longrightarrow \begin{array}{c} 9 \\ 7\overline{)63} \end{array}$$

If 9 × 6 = 54, then 54 ÷ 9 = 6.   If 7 × 9 = 63, then 63 ÷ 7 = 9.

Directions: Divide. Under each division problem, write the corresponding multiplication problem.

$$7\overline{)7}^{\,1} \qquad 6\overline{)24}^{\,4} \qquad 8\overline{)56}^{\,7}$$
7 × 1 = 7   6 × 4 = 24   8 × 7 = 56

$$5\overline{)30}^{\,6} \qquad 8\overline{)64}^{\,8} \qquad 6\overline{)12}^{\,2}$$
6 × 5 = 30   8 × 8 = 64   6 × 2 = 12

$$7\overline{)35}^{\,5} \qquad 8\overline{)24}^{\,3} \qquad 7\overline{)28}^{\,4}$$
7 × 5 = 35   8 × 3 = 24   7 × 4 = 28

100 Third Grade Skills

Page 60

Skill 28: Dividing Through 81 ÷ 9

Directions: Divide.

$$9\overline{)63}^{\,7} \qquad 9\overline{)81}^{\,9} \qquad 7\overline{)56}^{\,8} \qquad 5\overline{)35}^{\,7}$$

$$8\overline{)24}^{\,3} \qquad 9\overline{)18}^{\,2} \qquad 7\overline{)14}^{\,2} \qquad 7\overline{)21}^{\,3}$$

$$8\overline{)48}^{\,6} \qquad 9\overline{)45}^{\,5} \qquad 7\overline{)49}^{\,7} \qquad 8\overline{)16}^{\,2}$$

$$9\overline{)27}^{\,3} \qquad 9\overline{)9}^{\,1} \qquad 7\overline{)42}^{\,6} \qquad 9\overline{)27}^{\,3}$$

$$9\overline{)54}^{\,6} \qquad 8\overline{)8}^{\,1} \qquad 6\overline{)54}^{\,9} \qquad 8\overline{)40}^{\,5}$$

100 Third Grade Skills

Page 61

Answer Key

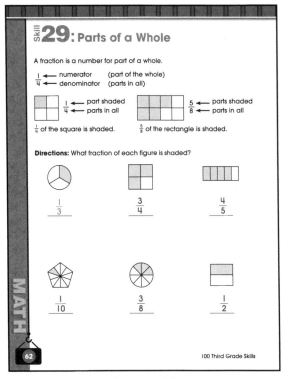

Page 62

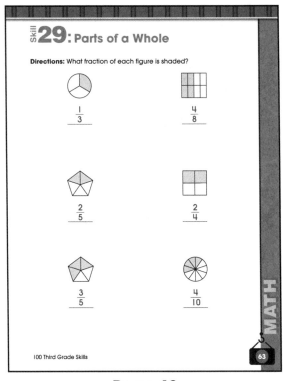

Page 63

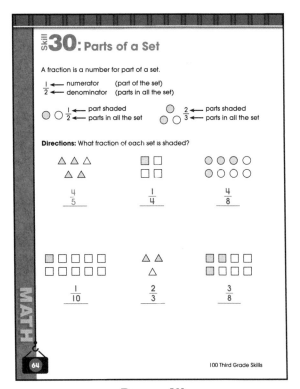

Page 64

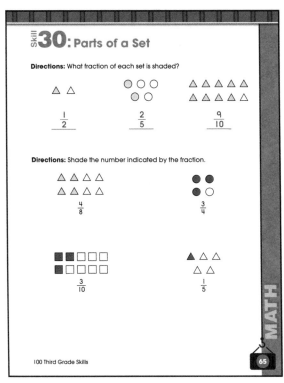

Page 65

Answer Key

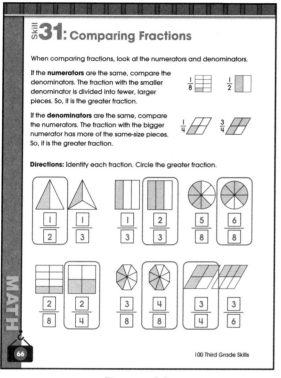

Page 66

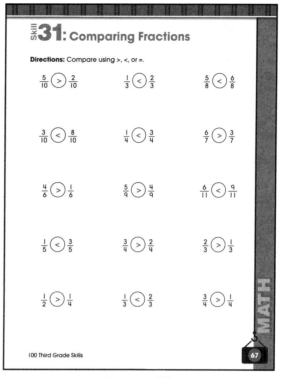

Page 67

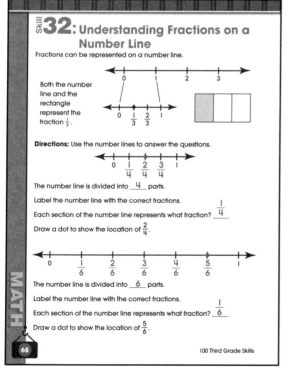

Page 68

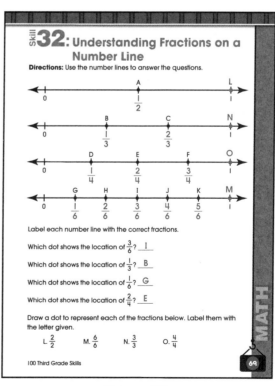

Page 69

Answer Key

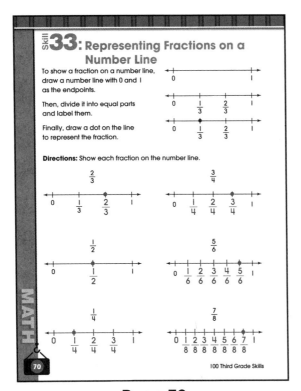

Page 70

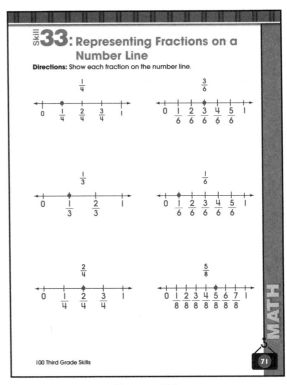

Page 71

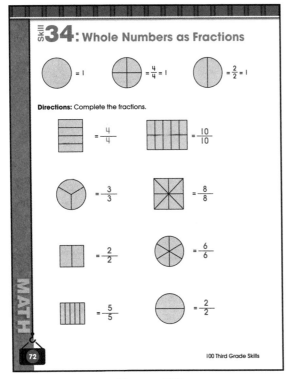

Page 72

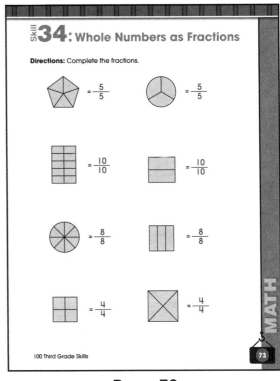

Page 73

Answer Key

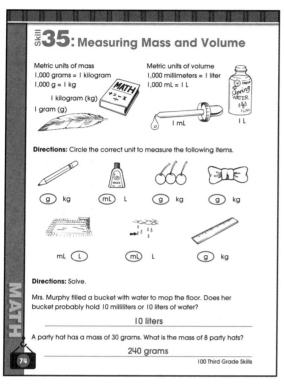

Page 74

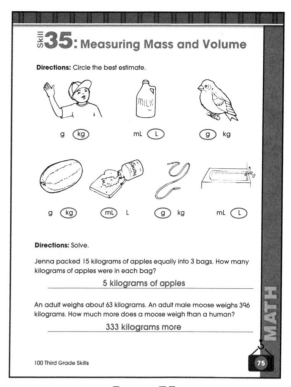

Page 75

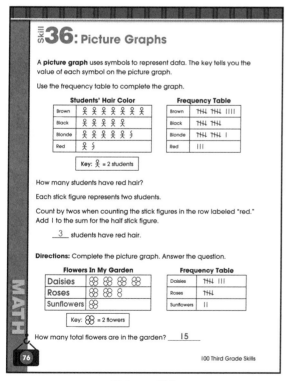

Page 76

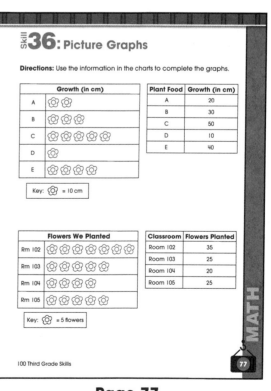

Page 77

Answer Key

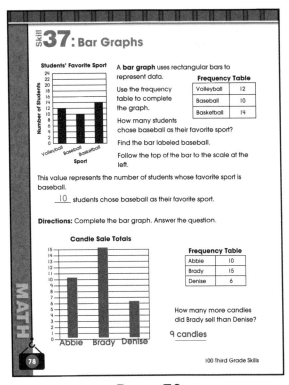

Page 78

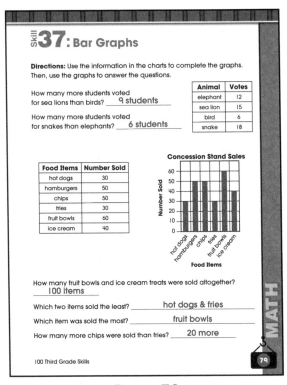

Page 79

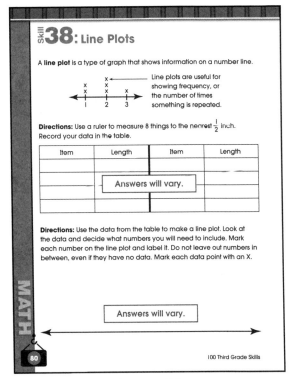

Page 80

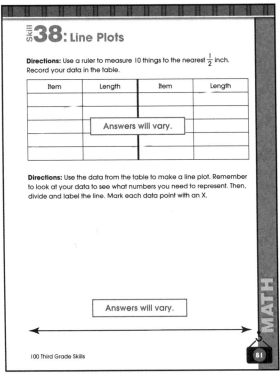

Page 81

Answer Key

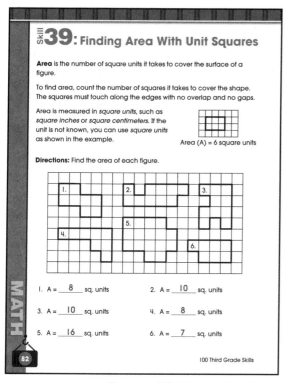

Skill 39: Finding Area With Unit Squares

Area is the number of square units it takes to cover the surface of a figure.

To find area, count the number of squares it takes to cover the shape. The squares must touch along the edges with no overlap and no gaps.

Area is measured in *square units*, such as *square inches* or *square centimeters*. If the unit is not known, you can use *square units* as shown in the example.

Area (A) = 6 square units

Directions: Find the area of each figure.

1. A = __8__ sq. units   2. A = __10__ sq. units

3. A = __10__ sq. units   4. A = __8__ sq. units

5. A = __16__ sq. units   6. A = __7__ sq. units

100 Third Grade Skills

Page 82

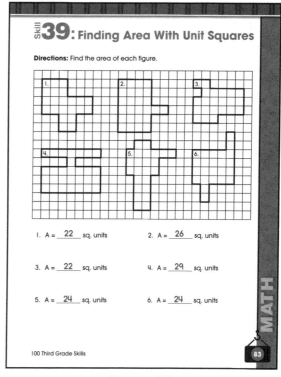

Skill 39: Finding Area With Unit Squares

Directions: Find the area of each figure.

1. A = __22__ sq. units   2. A = __26__ sq. units

3. A = __22__ sq. units   4. A = __29__ sq. units

5. A = __24__ sq. units   6. A = __24__ sq. units

100 Third Grade Skills

Page 83

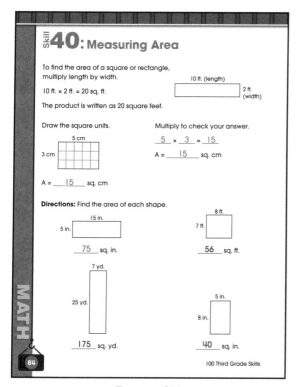

Skill 40: Measuring Area

To find the area of a square or rectangle, multiply length by width.

10 ft. × 2 ft. = 20 sq. ft.

10 ft. (length)
2 ft. (width)

The product is written as 20 square feet.

Draw the square units.

Multiply to check your answer.

__5__ × __3__ = __15__

A = __15__ sq. cm

5 cm
3 cm

A = __15__ sq. cm

Directions: Find the area of each shape.

15 in.
5 in.
__75__ sq. in.

8 ft.
7 ft.
__56__ sq. ft.

7 yd.
25 yd.
__175__ sq. yd.

5 in.
8 in.
__40__ sq. in.

100 Third Grade Skills

Page 84

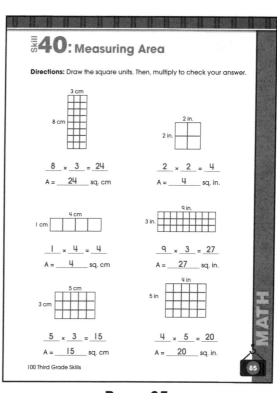

Skill 40: Measuring Area

Directions: Draw the square units. Then, multiply to check your answer.

3 cm
8 cm
__8__ × __3__ = __24__
A = __24__ sq. cm

2 in.
2 in.
__2__ × __2__ = __4__
A = __4__ sq. in.

4 cm
1 cm
__1__ × __4__ = __4__
A = __4__ sq. cm

9 in.
3 in.
__9__ × __3__ = __27__
A = __27__ sq. in.

5 cm
3 cm
__5__ × __3__ = __15__
A = __15__ sq. cm

4 in
5 in
__4__ × __5__ = __20__
A = __20__ sq. in.

100 Third Grade Skills

Page 85

Answer Key

Skill 41: Irregular Shapes

Divide the figure into recognizable shapes.

Find the area of each individual shape.

Then, add the areas together to find the total area of the shape.

Directions: Find the area of each figure.

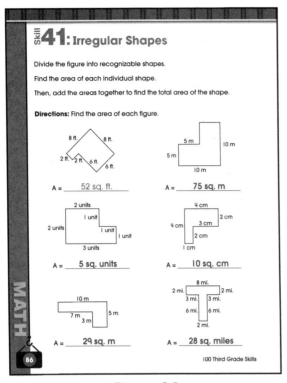

A = __52 sq. ft.__

A = __75 sq. m__

A = __5 sq. units__

A = __10 sq. cm__

A = __29 sq. m__

A = __28 sq. miles__

Page 86

Skill 41: Irregular Shapes

Directions: Find the area of each figure.

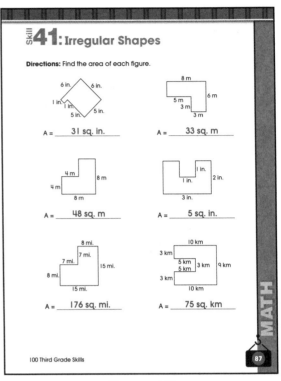

A = __31 sq. in.__

A = __33 sq. m__

A = __48 sq. m__

A = __5 sq. in.__

A = __176 sq. mi.__

A = __75 sq. km__

Page 87

Skill 42: Measuring Perimeter

Perimeter is the total distance around a given figure. To find the perimeter, add the lengths of the sides together.

Example: P = perimeter

P = 4 cm + 8 cm + 4 cm + 8 cm

P = 24 cm

Directions: Find the perimeter of each figure.

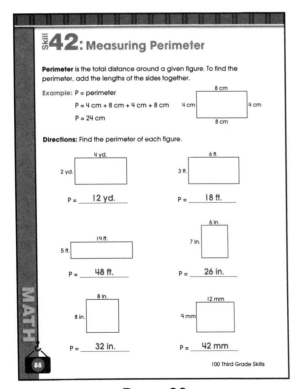

P = __12 yd.__

P = __18 ft.__

P = __48 ft.__

P = __26 in.__

P = __32 in.__

P = __42 mm__

Page 88

Skill 42: Measuring Perimeter

Directions: Find the perimeter of each figure.

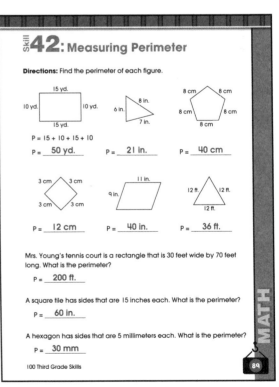

P = 15 + 10 + 15 + 10

P = __50 yd.__

P = __21 in.__

P = __40 cm__

P = __12 cm__

P = __40 in.__

P = __36 ft.__

Mrs. Young's tennis court is a rectangle that is 30 feet wide by 70 feet long. What is the perimeter?

P = __200 ft.__

A square tile has sides that are 15 inches each. What is the perimeter?

P = __60 in.__

A hexagon has sides that are 5 millimeters each. What is the perimeter?

P = __30 mm__

Page 89

Answer Key

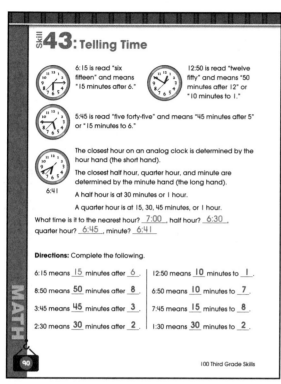

Skill 43: Telling Time

6:15 is read "six fifteen" and means "15 minutes after 6."

12:50 is read "twelve fifty" and means "50 minutes after 12" or "10 minutes to 1."

5:45 is read "five forty-five" and means "45 minutes after 5" or "15 minutes to 6."

The closest hour on an analog clock is determined by the hour hand (the short hand).

The closest half hour, quarter hour, and minute are determined by the minute hand (the long hand).

6:41

A half hour is at 30 minutes or 1 hour.

A quarter hour is at 15, 30, 45 minutes, or 1 hour.

What time is it to the nearest hour? __7:00__, half hour? __6:30__, quarter hour? __6:45__, minute? __6:41__

Directions: Complete the following.

6:15 means __15__ minutes after __6__. | 12:50 means __10__ minutes to __1__.
8:50 means __50__ minutes after __8__. | 6:50 means __10__ minutes to __7__.
3:45 means __45__ minutes after __3__. | 7:45 means __15__ minutes to __8__.
2:30 means __30__ minutes after __2__. | 1:30 means __30__ minutes to __2__.

90

100 Third Grade Skills

Page 90

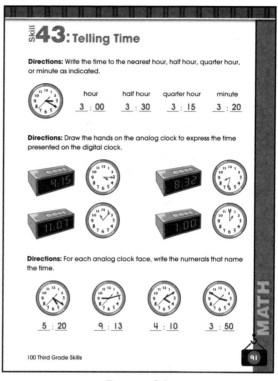

Skill 43: Telling Time

Directions: Write the time to the nearest hour, half hour, quarter hour, or minute as indicated.

	hour	half hour	quarter hour	minute
	__3__ : 00	__3__ : 30	__3__ : 15	__3__ : 20

Directions: Draw the hands on the analog clock to express the time presented on the digital clock.

4:15   8:32

11:07   1:00

Directions: For each analog clock face, write the numerals that name the time.

__5__ : __20__   __9__ : __13__   __4__ : __10__   __3__ : __50__

100 Third Grade Skills

91

Page 91

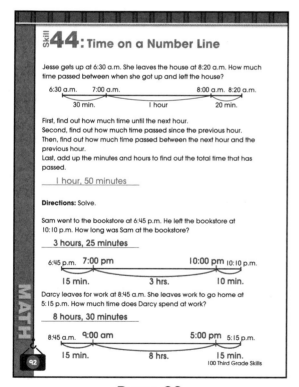

Skill 44: Time on a Number Line

Jesse gets up at 6:30 a.m. She leaves the house at 8:20 a.m. How much time passed between when she got up and left the house?

6:30 a.m.   7:00 a.m.   8:00 a.m. 8:20 a.m.
      30 min.   1 hour   20 min.

First, find out how much time until the next hour.
Second, find out how much time passed since the previous hour.
Then, find out how much time passed between the next hour and the previous hour.
Last, add up the minutes and hours to find out the total time that has passed.

__1 hour, 50 minutes__

Directions: Solve.

Sam went to the bookstore at 6:45 p.m. He left the bookstore at 10:10 p.m. How long was Sam at the bookstore?

__3 hours, 25 minutes__

6:45 p.m. 7:00 pm   10:00 pm 10:10 p.m.
      15 min.   3 hrs.   10 min.

Darcy leaves for work at 8:45 a.m. She leaves work to go home at 5:15 p.m. How much time does Darcy spend at work?

__8 hours, 30 minutes__

8:45 a.m. 9:00 am   5:00 pm 5:15 p.m.
      15 min.   8 hrs.   15 min.

92

100 Third Grade Skills

Page 92

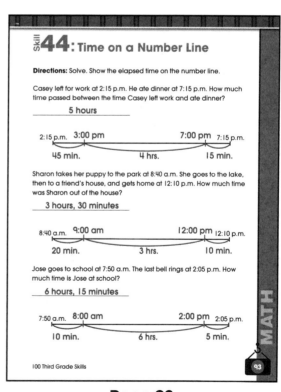

Skill 44: Time on a Number Line

Directions: Solve. Show the elapsed time on the number line.

Casey left for work at 2:15 p.m. He ate dinner at 7:15 p.m. How much time passed between the time Casey left work and ate dinner?

__5 hours__

2:15 p.m. 3:00 pm   7:00 pm 7:15 p.m.
      45 min.   4 hrs.   15 min.

Sharon takes her puppy to the park at 8:40 a.m. She goes to the lake, then to a friend's house, and gets home at 12:10 p.m. How much time was Sharon out of the house?

__3 hours, 30 minutes__

8:40 a.m. 9:00 am   12:00 pm 12:10 p.m.
      20 min.   3 hrs.   10 min.

Jose goes to school at 7:50 a.m. The last bell rings at 2:05 p.m. How much time is Jose at school?

__6 hours, 15 minutes__

7:50 a.m. 8:00 am   2:00 pm 2:05 p.m.
      10 min.   6 hrs.   5 min.

100 Third Grade Skills

93

Page 93

Answer Key

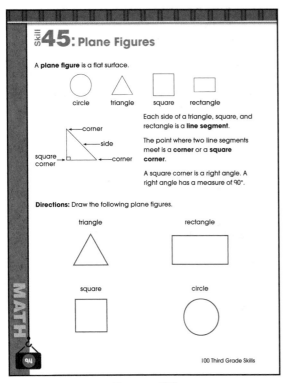

Page 94

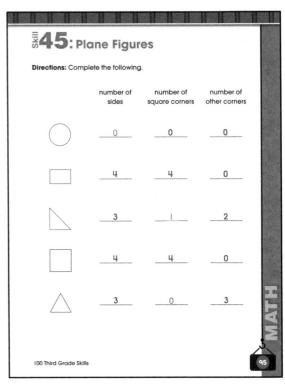

Page 95

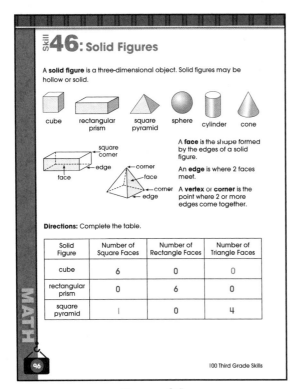

Page 96

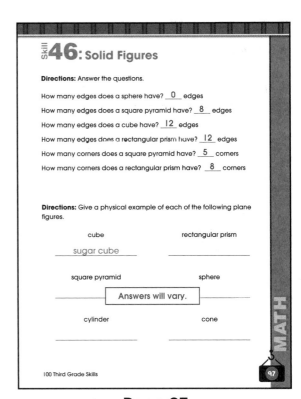

Page 97

100 Third Grade Skills

Answer Key

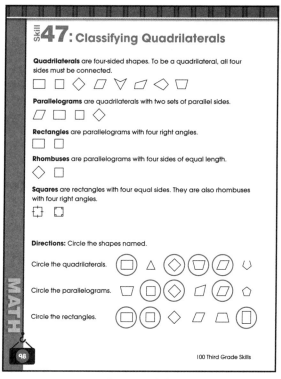

Page 98

Directions: Circle the shapes named. Then, answer the question.

Circle the rhombuses.

Circle the squares.

Which of the shapes defined above fits into all five categories?

___square___

Directions: Name each four-sided figure.

rectangle   rhombus   square   quadrilateral

Directions: How many sides or edges are there on these figures?

4   12   4   8

100 Third Grade Skills

Page 99

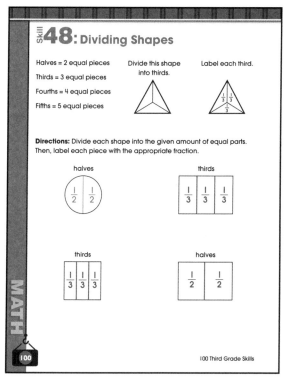

Page 100

Directions: Divide each shape into the given amount of equal parts. Then, label each piece with the appropriate fraction.

fourths

fifths

halves

fourths

fifths

thirds

halves

fourths

100 Third Grade Skills

Page 101

Answer Key

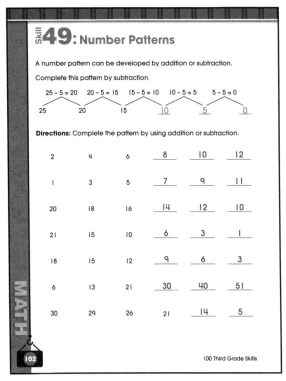

Page 102

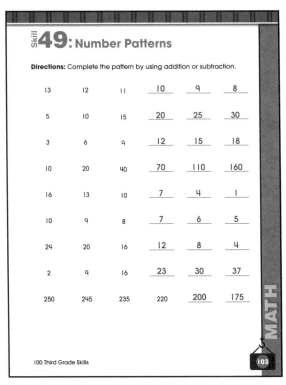

Page 103

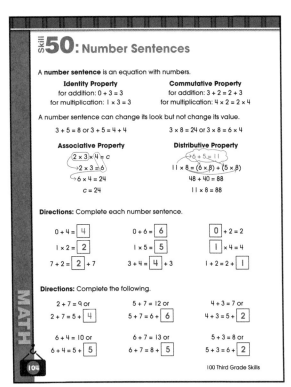

Page 104

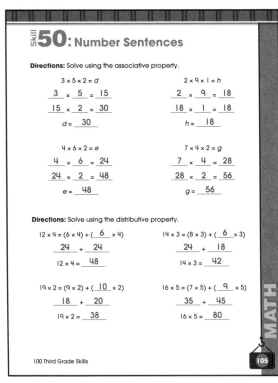

Page 105

Answer Key

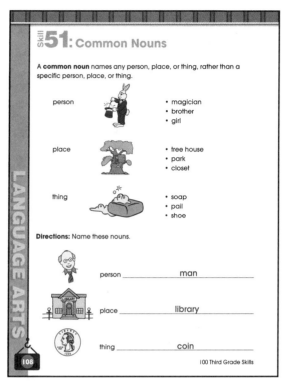

100 Third Grade Skills

Skill 51: Common Nouns

A **common noun** names any person, place, or thing, rather than a specific person, place, or thing.

person
- magician
- brother
- girl

place
- tree house
- park
- closet

thing
- soap
- pail
- shoe

Directions: Name these nouns.

person _____ man _____

place _____ library _____

thing _____ coin _____

Page 108

Skill 51: Common Nouns

Directions: Read the sentences below and write the common noun that you find in each sentence. The first one is done for you.

1. _____ socks _____ My socks do not match.

2. _____ bird _____ The bird could not fly.

3. _____ jelly beans _____ Ben likes to eat jelly beans.

4. _____ mother _____ I am going to meet my mother.

5. _____ lake _____ We will go swimming in the lake tomorrow.

6. _____ flowers _____ I hope the flowers will grow quickly.

7. _____ eggs _____ We colored eggs together.

8. _____ bicycle _____ It is easy to ride a bicycle.

9. _____ coat _____ Please hand me my coat.

100 Third Grade Skills

Page 109

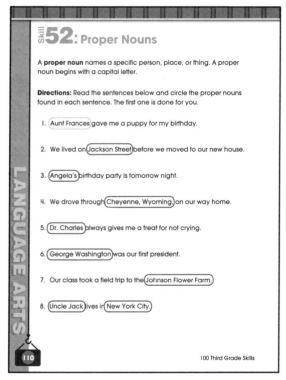

Skill 52: Proper Nouns

A **proper noun** names a specific person, place, or thing. A proper noun begins with a capital letter.

Directions: Read the sentences below and circle the proper nouns found in each sentence. The first one is done for you.

1. (Aunt Frances) gave me a puppy for my birthday.

2. We lived on (Jackson Street) before we moved to our new house.

3. (Angela's) birthday party is tomorrow night.

4. We drove through (Cheyenne, Wyoming) on our way home.

5. (Dr. Charles) always gives me a treat for not crying.

6. (George Washington) was our first president.

7. Our class took a field trip to the (Johnson Flower Farm.)

8. (Uncle Jack) lives in (New York City.)

100 Third Grade Skills

Page 110

Skill 52: Proper Nouns

Directions: Write about you! Write a proper noun for each category below. Capitalize the first letter of each proper noun.

1. Your first name: _____

2. Your last name: _____

3. Your street: _____

4. Your city: _____   Answers will vary.

5. Your state: _____

6. Your country: _____

7. Your school: _____

8. Your best friend: _____

100 Third Grade Skills

Page 111

Answer Key

Skill 53: Abstract Nouns

Abstract nouns are nouns that you can't experience with your five senses. They are feelings, concepts, and ideas. Some examples are **friendship, childhood, bravery, hope,** and **pride.**

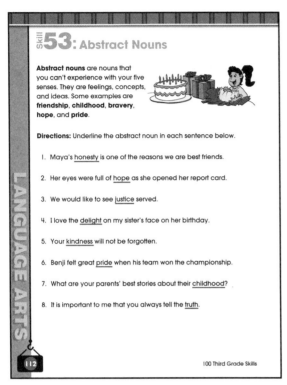

Directions: Underline the abstract noun in each sentence below.

1. Maya's <u>honesty</u> is one of the reasons we are best friends.

2. Her eyes were full of <u>hope</u> as she opened her report card.

3. We would like to see <u>justice</u> served.

4. I love the <u>delight</u> on my sister's face on her birthday.

5. Your <u>kindness</u> will not be forgotten.

6. Benji felt great <u>pride</u> when his team won the championship.

7. What are your parents' best stories about their <u>childhood</u>?

8. It is important to me that you always tell the <u>truth.</u>

Page 112

Skill 53: Abstract Nouns

Directions: Fill in each blank below with an abstract noun from the box.

wisdom	joy	knowledge
courage	freedom	love

1. You can see the ___love___ this father has for his son.

2. It took great ___courage___ to rebuild after the hurricane.

3. Uncle Zane's ___knowledge___ of birds amazes me.

4. The room was filled with ___joy___ when Will found his lost puppy.

5. It would be great to have the ___freedom___ to travel the world.

6. Grandpa has the ___wisdom___ that comes with a long life.

Page 113

Skill 54: Plural Nouns

A noun that names one thing, like **house**, is **singular**. A noun that names more than one thing, like **houses**, is **plural**.

To make most words plural, add **s**.

Example: one book — two books   one tree — four trees

To make words that end in **s, ss, x, sh,** and **ch** plural, add **es**.

Example: one fox — two foxes   one bush — three bushes

Directions: Add **s** or **es** to make each word plural.

1. pencil ___pencils___
2. peach ___peaches___
3. class ___classes___
4. ax ___axes___
5. bush ___bushes___
6. crash ___crashes___

To make a word that ends in **y** plural, change the **y** to **i** and add **es**.

Example: pony — ponies

Directions: Write the plural form of each noun.

1. baby ___babies___
2. bunny ___bunnies___
3. cherry ___cherries___
4. kitty ___kitties___
5. sky ___skies___
6. candy ___candies___

Page 114

Skill 54: Plural Nouns

To make **plural nouns:**

Add **s** to most singular nouns ending in a vowel and the letter **o**.

Example: rodeo — rodeos

Add **es** to most singular nouns ending in a consonant and the letter **o**.

Example: tomato — tomatoes

Change the **f** to **v** and add **es** to singular nouns ending in **f**.

Example: leaf — leaves

Directions: Circle the correct plural form of each noun.

1. avocado	(avocados)	avocatos	avocatose
2. wolf	wolfs	(wolves)	wolvs
3. mosquito	(mosquitoes)	mosquitoz	mosquitos
4. halo	(halos)	haloes	haloz
5. knife	(knives)	knifs	knifes
6. zero	(zeroes)	zeros	zeroz
7. elf	elfs	(elves)	elfz
8. volcano	(volcanoes)	volcanos	volcanoese
9. shelf	shelfs	shelvs	(shelves)
10. hoof	(hooves)	hoofs	hoofes

Page 115

Answer Key

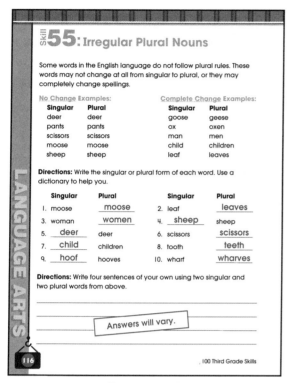

Skill 55: Irregular Plural Nouns

Some words in the English language do not follow plural rules. These words may not change at all from singular to plural, or they may completely change spellings.

No Change Examples:

Singular	Plural
deer	deer
pants	pants
scissors	scissors
moose	moose
sheep	sheep

Complete Change Examples:

Singular	Plural
goose	geese
ox	oxen
man	men
child	children
leaf	leaves

Directions: Write the singular or plural form of each word. Use a dictionary to help you.

	Singular	Plural		Singular	Plural
1.	moose	moose	2.	leaf	leaves
3.	woman	women	4.	sheep	sheep
5.	deer	deer	6.	scissors	scissors
7.	child	children	8.	tooth	teeth
9.	hoof	hooves	10.	wharf	wharves

Directions: Write four sentences of your own using two singular and two plural words from above.

Answers will vary.

116

100 Third Grade Skills

Page 116

Skill 55: Irregular Plural Nouns

Directions: Match each phrase below to the correct plural form. Write the letter on the line.

1. __b__ one bison   **a.** fifty bisons   **b.** fifty bison
2. __a__ one die   **a.** six dice   **b.** six dies
3. __a__ one offspring   **a.** many offspring   **b.** many offsprings
4. __a__ the trout   **a.** hundreds of trout   **b.** hundreds of trouts
5. __a__ one species   **a.** eight species   **b.** eight specieses
6. __b__ the goose   **a.** four gooses   **b.** four geese
7. __b__ one series   **a.** three serieses   **b.** three series
8. __b__ a child   **a.** most childs   **b.** most children

100 Third Grade Skills

117

Page 117

Skill 56: Singular Possessive Nouns

To make a singular noun show **possession**, or ownership, add an apostrophe (') and the letter **s**.

Example: Deandre — **Deandre's** hiking shoes are muddy.
tree — The **tree's** limbs are heavy with snow.

Directions: Change each noun to its possessive form.

1.	snake	snake's	2.	lizard	lizard's
3.	bottle	bottle's	4.	flower	flower's
5.	bird	bird's	6.	pirate	pirate's

Directions: Write a sentence using the possessive form of each word.

1. Bailey _____

2. car _____

3. bug _____ Answers will vary.

4. flower _____

5. bed _____

118

100 Third Grade Skills

Page 118

Skill 56: Singular Possessive Nouns

Directions: Circle the correct possessive noun in each sentence and write it in the blank. The first one is done for you.

1. One ____girl's____ dad is a doctor.
   (girl's) girls'

2. The ____cat's____ tail is long.
   (cat's) cats'

3. One ____boy's____ soccer ball is new.
   (boy's) boys'

4. A ____waitress's____ apron is white.
   waitresses' (waitress's)

5. My ____grandma's____ apple pie is the best!
   (grandma's) grandmas'

6. The ____child's____ hair is pretty.
   (child's) childs'

7. This ____dog's____ collar is green.
   (dog's) dogs'

8. The ____cow's____ tail is short.
   (cow's) cows'

100 Third Grade Skills

119

Page 119

Answer Key

Skill 57: Plural Possessive Nouns

To make a plural noun ending in **s** show **possession** or ownership, add an apostrophe (') after the letter **s**.

Example: boys — The **boys'** mother took them to the skate park.

If the plural noun does not end in **s**, add an apostrophe (') and the letter **s**.

Example: men — The **men's** fitting room is on the left.

Directions: Change each plural noun to its possessive form.

1. cups — cups'
2. children — children's
3. hamburgers — hamburgers'
4. parents — parents'
5. french fries — french fries'
6. milkshakes — milkshakes'
7. workers — workers'
8. sundaes — sundaes'
9. straws — straws'
10. fish — fish's

100 Third Grade Skills

120

Page 120

Skill 57: Plural Possessive Nouns

Directions: Write a sentence using the possessive form of each plural noun.

1. girls _____
2. women _____
3. shirts _____
4. cookies _____
5. brothers _____
6. igloos _____
7. explorers _____
8. bears _____
9. peanuts _____

Answers will vary.

100 Third Grade Skills

121

Page 121

Skill 58: Pronouns

A **pronoun** is a word that takes the place of a noun.

Example: **he, she, it, they, him, them, her, him**

Directions: Read each sentence. Write the pronoun that takes the place of each noun. The first one is done for you.

1. The **monkey** dropped the banana. — It
2. **Dad** washed the car last night. — He
3. **Dawn and Greg** took a walk in the park. — They
4. **Jessica** spent the night at her friend's house. — She
5. The basketball **players** lost their game. — They
6. **Lionel Messi** is a great soccer player. — He
7. The **parrot** can say five different words. — It
8. **Heather** wrote a report in class today. — She
9. They planned a party for **Naomi**. — her
10. Everyone in the class was happy for **Brad**. — him

100 Third Grade Skills

122

Page 122

Skill 58: Pronouns

Use the pronouns **I** and **we** when talking about the person or people doing the action.

Example: **I** can skate.
We can skate.

Use the pronouns **me** and **us** when talking about the person or people receiving the action.

Example: They gave **me** the skates.
They gave **us** the skates.

Directions: Circle the correct pronoun and write it in the blank. The first one is done for you.

1. __We__ are going to the show together. — (We) Us
2. __I__ am finished with my history project. — (I) Me
3. Andrew passed the salt to __me__. — (me) I
4. They ate lunch with __us__ yesterday. — we (us)
5. __We__ had a pool party in our backyard. — Us (We)
6. They told __us__ the good news. — (us) we
7. Jake and __I__ went to the movies. — me (I)
8. She is taking __me__ with her to the concert. — I (me)

100 Third Grade Skills

123

Page 123

236

100 Third Grade Skills

Answer Key

Skill 59: Subject and Object Pronouns

A **subject pronoun** takes the place of a noun in the subject of a sentence.

An **object pronoun** takes the place of a noun that follows a verb or a word such as **to, from, of, at, with,** or **by.**

Subject Pronouns						
I	you	he	she	it	we	they

Object Pronouns						
me	you	him	her	it	us	you	them

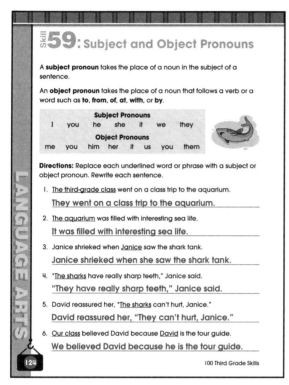

Directions: Replace each underlined word or phrase with a subject or object pronoun. Rewrite each sentence.

1. The third-grade class went on a class trip to the aquarium.
   They went on a class trip to the aquarium.

2. The aquarium was filled with interesting sea life.
   It was filled with interesting sea life.

3. Janice shrieked when Janice saw the shark tank.
   Janice shrieked when she saw the shark tank.

4. "The sharks have really sharp teeth," Janice said.
   "They have really sharp teeth," Janice said.

5. David reassured her, "The sharks can't hurt, Janice."
   David reassured her, "They can't hurt, Janice."

6. Our class believed David because David is the tour guide.
   We believed David because he is the tour guide.

124

100 Third Grade Skills

Page 124

Skill 59: Subject and Object Pronouns

Directions: Read the sentences below. Cross out the incorrect pronouns. Then, write the correct pronouns above them.

1. The students in Ms. Curry's class are going
   They
   on a field trip. ~~Them~~ are going to the museum.

2. Ms. Curry told ~~we~~ **us** that the museum is her favorite field trip.

3. The bus will leave at 8:30 in the morning. ~~She~~ **It** will be parked in the school's west lot.

4. Casey and Allison will sit together. ~~Them~~ **They** are best friends.

5. Ibrahim or Peter might sit with ~~I~~. **me**

6. The Goose Creek museum is not far away. It did not take ~~we~~ **us** long to drive to ~~him~~. **it**

7. Michael forgot to bring his lunch. Ms. Curry gave ~~he~~ **him** half of her sandwich and an apple.

8. ~~Me~~ **I** loved seeing all the fossils.

100 Third Grade Skills

125

Page 125

Skill 60: Verbs

A **verb** is the action word in a sentence. It is the word that tells what something does or that something exists.

Example: run, jump, skip

Directions: Draw a box around the verb in each sentence below.

1. Spiders spin webs of silk.
2. A spider waits in the center of the web for its meals.
3. A spider sinks its sharp fangs into insects.
4. Spiders eat many insects.
5. Spiders make their nests with silk.
6. Female spiders wrap silk around their eggs to protect them.

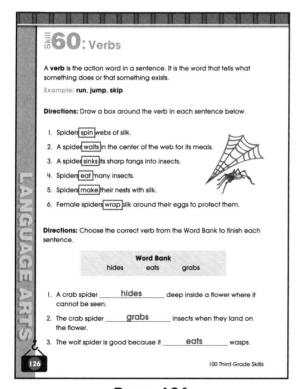

Directions: Choose the correct verb from the Word Bank to finish each sentence.

Word Bank		
hides	eats	grabs

1. A crab spider **hides** deep inside a flower where it cannot be seen.

2. The crab spider **grabs** insects when they land on the flower.

3. The wolf spider is good because it **eats** wasps.

126

100 Third Grade Skills

Page 126

Skill 60: Verbs

Directions: Write an action word from the Word Bank in each blank.

Word Bank			
dances	eats	rides	shoots

1. Brady **rides** his new, red bike.
2. The girl **dances** on the stage.
3. Coby **shoots** the arrow at the target.
4. Judy **eats** pumpkin pie.

Directions: Write three sentences using verbs from the Word Bank.

Word Bank				
creates	hammers	builds	mows	scrubs

1. _____

2. _____   Answers will vary.

3. _____

100 Third Grade Skills

127

Page 127

Answer Key

Skill 61: Linking Verbs

A **linking verb** connects the noun to a descriptive word. A linking verb is often a form of the verb **be**.

Directions: The linking verb is underlined in each sentence. Circle the two words that the linking verb connects.

Example: The cat is fat.

1. My favorite food is lasagna.
2. The car was blue.
3. I am tired.
4. Books are fun!
5. The garden is beautiful.
6. The pear was juicy.
7. The garage is large.
8. Rabbits are furry.

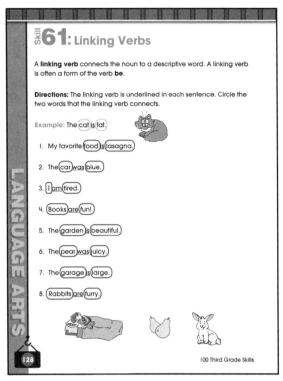

128   100 Third Grade Skills

Page 128

Skill 61: Linking Verbs

Directions: Write the correct linking verb (**am, is,** or **are**) to complete each sentence.

1. We ___are___ going to the pool today.
2. The day ___is___ perfect for soccer.
3. The students ___are___ happy.
4. She ___is___ the one who organized the party.
5. He ___is___ a good student.
6. I ___am___ tired from hiking all day.
7. They ___are___ going to the movies after school.
8. Mr. Johnson ___is___ the teacher.
9. I ___am___ excited about our trip!
10. You ___are___ my best friend.

100 Third Grade Skills   129

Page 129

Skill 62: The Verb Be

Most verbs name an action. The verb **be** is different. It tells about someone or something. **Am, is,** and **are** are forms of the verb **be**.

Use **is** with one person, place, or thing.

Example: Mrs. Jones **is** my principal.

Use **are** with more than one person, place, or thing or with the word **you**.

Example: We **are** studying presidents.   You **are** excited.

Use **am** with the word **I**.

Example: I **am** sad today.

Directions: Fill in each blank with the correct form of the verb **be** (**is, am,** or **are**).

1. My dog ___is___ brown.
2. My favorite color ___is___ green.
3. We ___are___ baking a cake today.
4. I ___am___ going to the movies on Saturday.
5. My friends ___are___ going with me.
6. What ___is___ your cell phone number?

130   100 Third Grade Skills

Page 130

Skill 62: The Verb Be

Directions: Fill in each blank with the correct form of the verb **be** (**am, is,** or **are**).

1. You ___are___ standing on my foot.
2. I ___am___ going for a walk.
3. The firefighter ___is___ driving the engine.
4. Chandra and I ___are___ playing basketball.
5. The band ___is___ marching in the parade.
6. Denver ___is___ east of San Francisco.
7. My parents ___are___ in Hawaii.
8. Who ___is___ coming camping with me next weekend?
9. Julia and Ben ___are___ in third grade.
10. I ___am___ cooking potatoes and a pie for Thanksgiving.
11. You and Max ___are___ winning an award.

100 Third Grade Skills   131

Page 131

Answer Key

Skill 63: Subject-Verb Agreement

When a sentence has a singular subject, the verb ends with **s** or **es**.

Add **s** to most regular verbs that have a single subject.

Example: The *boat* sails close to shore.

Add **es** to regular verbs that have a single subject and end in **sh, ch, s, x,** and **z**.

Example: *Gran* kisses us good-bye.

When the subject is plural, the verb does not end with **s** or **es**.

Example: The *kittens* sleep on the sofa.

Directions: Read the paragraph below. Add or delete **s** or **es** from the verbs so that they agree with their subjects. Use this symbol (^) to add a letter or letters.

es
Mr. Huff wash^his car on Saturdays. Adam and Amy help him. Mr.
s
Huff sprays the car with warm water and soap. He scrub the car with

a big sponge. The children clean the windshield and the mirrors. They
es   s
use clean, soft rags. Adam wax^the beautiful red car. It shine^in the
s
sunlight. Mr. Huff take^Adam and Amy for a drive in the shiny car every

Saturday afternoon. Then, they walk in the park.

Page 132

Skill 63: Subject-Verb Agreement

Directions: Read each sentence below. Then, read the pair of verbs in parentheses ( ). Choose the correct verb form. Write it on the line.

1. Emily and Mateo _____ toss _____ a ball in the backyard. (toss, tosses)

2. The Smiths _____ carve _____ their pumpkins every autumn. (carve, carves)

3. My little brother _____ brushes _____ the dog with a new brush. (brush, brushes)

4. Brian _____ runs _____ five miles a day when he is in training for a race. (run, runs)

5. The blender _____ mixes _____ the ingredients. (mix, mixes)

6. The Thompsons _____ camp _____ near a snowy mountain every winter. (camp, camps)

7. The shaggy Irish setter _____ catches _____ the ball each time I throw it. (catch, catches)

8. Grandma Stella _____ lives _____ about one hour away. (live, lives)

Page 133

Skill 64: Helping Verbs

A **helping verb** is a word used with an action verb.

Example: **might, shall,** and **are**

They **are** meeting us at noon. Harry **might** ask your opinion.

Directions: Finish each sentence with a helping verb from the Word Bank. The first one is done for you.

Word Bank

can	could	must	might
may	would	should	will
shall	did	does	do
had	have	has	am
are	were	is	
be	being	been	

1. Tomorrow, I _____ might _____ play soccer.
2. Mom _____ buy my new dress tonight.
3. Yesterday, my new books _____ ripped by the cat.
4. I _____ _____ go to the mall.
5. She usually _____ _____ football. *(Answers will vary.)*
6. But, she _____ go with me because I am her friend.
7. She _____ promised to watch the entire football game.
8. He _____ helped me with my homework.
9. I _____ spell a lot better because of his help.
10. Maybe I _____ finish the semester at the top of my class.

Page 134

Skill 64: Helping Verbs

Common Helping Verbs

am	can	does	is	shall	will
are	could	had	may	should	would
be	did	has	might	was	
been	do	have	must	were	

Directions: Underline the action verb in each sentence. Then, choose the best helping verb and write it on the line.

1. Jasmine's family _____ is _____ organizing a neighborhood recycling project. (is had are)

2. They _____ are _____ talking to their neighbors. (is may are)

3. Mr. Chang's children _____ will _____ look for old newspapers and magazines. (will do were)

4. The Benson family _____ is _____ collecting plastic bottles. (should is did)

5. Jackie _____ might _____ open a lemonade stand to make some money. (have was might)

6. Mrs. Zane said she _____ would _____ drive us to the recycling center. (would be are)

7. We _____ must _____ respect our planet. (have must are)

Page 135

Answer Key

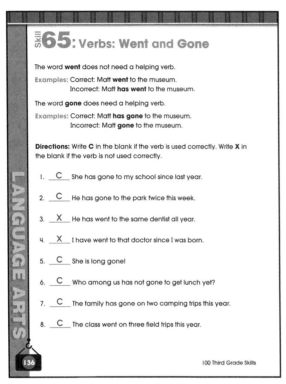

Skill 65: Verbs: Went and Gone

The word **went** does not need a helping verb.

Examples: Correct: Matt **went** to the museum.
Incorrect: Matt **has went** to the museum.

The word **gone** does need a helping verb.

Examples: Correct: Matt **has gone** to the museum.
Incorrect: Matt **gone** to the museum.

Directions: Write **C** in the blank if the verb is used correctly. Write **X** in the blank if the verb is not used correctly.

1. __C__ She has gone to my school since last year.
2. __C__ He has gone to the park twice this week.
3. __X__ He has went to the same dentist all year.
4. __X__ I have went to that doctor since I was born.
5. __C__ She is long gone!
6. __C__ Who among us has not gone to get lunch yet?
7. __C__ The family has gone on two camping trips this year.
8. __C__ The class went on three field trips this year.

136   100 Third Grade Skills

Page 136

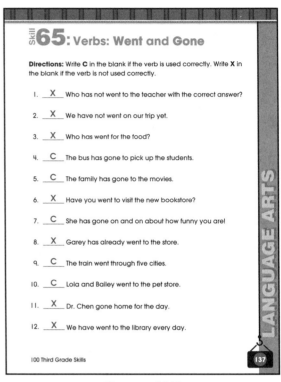

Skill 65: Verbs: Went and Gone

Directions: Write **C** in the blank if the verb is used correctly. Write **X** in the blank if the verb is not used correctly.

1. __X__ Who has not went to the teacher with the correct answer?
2. __X__ We have not went on our trip yet.
3. __X__ Who has went for the food?
4. __C__ The bus has gone to pick up the students.
5. __C__ The family has gone to the movies.
6. __X__ Have you went to visit the new bookstore?
7. __C__ She has gone on and on about how funny you are!
8. __X__ Garey has already went to the store.
9. __C__ The train went through five cities.
10. __C__ Lola and Bailey went to the pet store.
11. __X__ Dr. Chen gone home for the day.
12. __X__ We have went to the library every day.

100 Third Grade Skills   137

Page 137

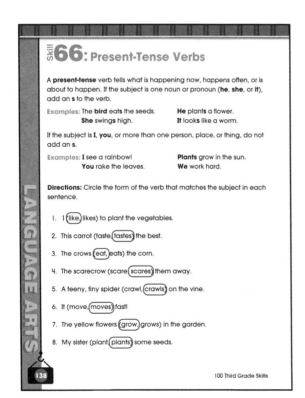

Skill 66: Present-Tense Verbs

A **present-tense** verb tells what is happening now, happens often, or is about to happen. If the subject is one noun or pronoun (**he**, **she**, or **it**), add an **s** to the verb.

Examples: The **bird** eats the seeds.   **He** plants a flower.
She swings high.   **It** looks like a worm.

If the subject is **I**, **you**, or more than one person, place, or thing, do not add an **s**.

Examples: **I** see a rainbow!   **Plants** grow in the sun.
You rake the leaves.   **We** work hard.

Directions: Circle the form of the verb that matches the subject in each sentence.

1. I (like, likes) to plant the vegetables.
2. This carrot (taste, tastes) the best.
3. The crows (eat, eats) the corn.
4. The scarecrow (scare, scares) them away.
5. A teeny, tiny spider (crawl, crawls) on the vine.
6. It (move, moves) fast!
7. The yellow flowers (grow, grows) in the garden.
8. My sister (plant, plants) some seeds.

138   100 Third Grade Skills

Page 138

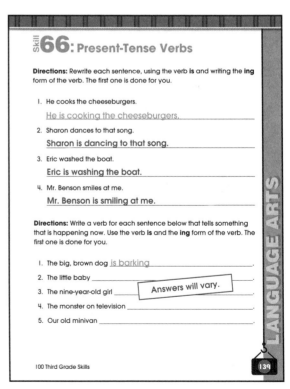

Skill 66: Present-Tense Verbs

Directions: Rewrite each sentence, using the verb **is** and writing the **ing** form of the verb. The first one is done for you.

1. He cooks the cheeseburgers.
   He is cooking the cheeseburgers.
2. Sharon dances to that song.
   Sharon is dancing to that song.
3. Eric washed the boat.
   Eric is washing the boat.
4. Mr. Benson smiles at me.
   Mr. Benson is smiling at me.

Directions: Write a verb for each sentence below that tells something that is happening now. Use the verb **is** and the **ing** form of the verb. The first one is done for you.

1. The big, brown dog is barking
2. The little baby _____
3. The nine-year-old girl _____   Answers will vary.
4. The monster on television _____
5. Our old minivan _____

100 Third Grade Skills   139

Page 139

Answer Key

Skill **67**: Past-Tense Verbs

When you write about something that already happened, add **ed** to most verbs. For some verbs that have a short vowel and end in one consonant, double the consonant before adding **ed**.

Examples: He hug**ged** his pillow.   The dog grab**bed** the stick.

To make many verbs past tense, add **ed**.

Examples: cook + ed = cooked   wish + ed = wished

When a verb ends in a **silent e**, add only **d**.

Examples: hope + ed = hoped

When a verb ends in **y** after a consonant, change the **y** to **i** and add **ed**.

Example: hurry + ed = hurried

When a verb ends in a single consonant after a single short vowel, double the final consonant before adding **ed**.

Example: stop + ed = stopped

Directions: Use the verb from the first sentence or clause to complete the second sentence. Change the verb in the second sentence to the past tense. Double the consonant and add **ed**. The first one is done for you.

1. We skip to school.

    Yesterday, we _____skipped_____ the whole way.

2. It is not nice to grab things.

    When you _____grabbed_____ my apple, I felt mad.

3. Did anyone hug you today?

    Mom _____hugged_____ me this morning.

LANGUAGE ARTS

Page 140

Skill **67**: Past-Tense Verbs

Directions: Use the verb from the first sentence or clause to complete the second sentence. Change the verb in the second sentence to the past tense. Double the consonant and add **ed**.

1. We plan our vacations every year.

    Last year, we _____planned_____ to go to the mountains.

2. Is it my turn to stir the pot?

    You _____stirred_____ it last time.

3. Let's clap for Andy, just like we _____clapped_____ for Amy.

Directions: Rewrite each verb in the past tense. The first one is done for you.

1. call	called	2. copy	copied
3. frown	frowned	4. smile	smiled
5. live	lived	6. talk	talked
7. name	named	8. list	listed
9. spy	spied	10. phone	phoned
11. bake	baked	12. type	typed

LANGUAGE ARTS

Page 141

Skill **68**: Future-Tense Verbs

The **future tense** of a verb tells about something that has not happened yet but will happen in the future. **Will** or **shall** are usually used with future tense.

Directions: Change the verb tense in each sentence to future tense. The first one is done for you.

1. She cooks dinner.

    She will cook dinner.

2. He plays soccer.

    He will play soccer.

3. She bikes to the bank.

    She will bike to the bank.

4. I remember to vote.

    I will remember to vote.

5. Jack mows the lawn every week.

    Jack will mow the lawn every week.

6. We go on vacation soon.

    We will go on vacation soon.

LANGUAGE ARTS

Page 142

Skill **68**: Future-Tense Verbs

Directions: On the line, write **PA** if a sentence takes place in the past. Write **PR** if it takes place in the present. Then, rewrite each sentence in the future tense.

Example: _PA_ The play ended at 9:00.

    The play will end at 9:00.

1. _PA_ The dog barked at the loud truck.

    The dog will bark at the loud truck.

2. _PR_ The gardener picks flowers from her wildflower garden.

    The gardener will pick flowers from her wildflower garden.

3. _PR_ The frog pulls a worm from the pond.

    The frog will pull a worm from the pond.

4. _PA_ A ladybug landed on Layla's shoulder.

    A ladybug will land on Layla's shoulder.

Directions: Write a sentence about somewhere you will go or something you will do in the future. Underline the verb.

_____ Answers will vary. _____

LANGUAGE ARTS

Page 143

Answer Key

Skill 69: Adjectives

A word that **describes** a noun is called an **adjective**.

Adjectives tell:

What Kind: **white** egg	**small** car	**messy** room
How Many: **five** flags	**many** books	**a half-dozen** donuts
Which One: **those** ducklings	**that** lamp	**this** bowl

Directions: Write an adjective that could describe each thing.

1. cereal _____
2. shoes _____
3. cat _____
4. test _____
5. boys
6. frog _____
7. sisters _____
8. bikes _____
9. ice cream _____

Answers will vary.

Page 144

Skill 69: Adjectives

Directions: Finish each sentence using an adjective from the Word Bank.

Word Bank

green   soft   ugly   expensive   thousands   warty

1. The _____soft_____ pillows were very _____expensive_____ to buy because they were made of _____thousands_____ of downy feathers.

2. The _____green_____, _____warty_____ frog was so _____ugly_____ that everybody was afraid to look at him.

Directions: Finish each sentence using an adjective from the Word Bank.

Word Bank

hungry   beautiful   delicate   tall   loud   scary

1. Brown bears can be very _____scary_____ when they are _____hungry_____. They stand up _____tall_____ and let out _____loud_____ growls.

2. Tulips are _____beautiful_____ flowers and quite _____delicate_____. Their petals feel like smooth velvet.

Page 145

Skill 70: Comparative Adjectives and Adverbs

Add the suffix **er** to an adjective to compare two things.
Example: My feet are **large**.
Your feet are **larger** than my feet.

When a one-syllable adjective ends in a single consonant and the vowel is short, double the final consonant before adding **er**. When a word ends in two or more consonants, add **er**.
Examples: big — bigger (single consonant)
bold — bolder (two consonants)

When an adjective ends in **y**, change the **y** to **i** before adding **er**.
Example: easy — easier

Add the suffix **est** to adjectives to compare more than two things.
Example: My glass is **full**.   Your glass is **fuller**.   His glass is **fullest**.

When a one-syllable adjective ends in a single consonant and the vowel sound is short, double the final consonant before adding **est**.
Examples: big — biggest (short vowel)
steep — steepest (long vowel)

When an adjective ends in **y**, change the **y** to **i** before adding **est**.
Example: easy — easiest

Directions: Use the correct rule to add **er** to the words below for numbers 1–4. Then, use the correct rule to add **est** to the words below for numbers 5–8.

1. fast _____faster_____
2. thin _____thinner_____
3. long _____longer_____
4. clean _____cleaner_____
5. pretty _____prettiest_____
6. early _____earliest_____
7. quick _____quickest_____
8. trim _____trimmest_____

Page 146

Skill 70: Comparative Adjectives and Adverbs

To make a comparison using adverbs that end in **ly**, use the words *more* or *most*.

Example: Dawn read the book *more slowly* than Kim.
My sister sang *most beautifully* of all the girls in her class.

Directions: Fill in the spaces in the chart with the correct adverbs. Remember that some comparative adverbs need to be used with the words *more* or *most*.

slowly	more slowly	most slowly
fast	faster	fastest
skillfully	more skillfully	most skillfully
happily	more happily	most happily
patiently	more patiently	most patiently
late	later	latest
safely	more safely	most safely
playfully	more playfully	most playfully

Page 147

Answer Key

Page 148

Skill 71: Adverbs

Like adjectives, **adverbs** are describing words. They describe verbs. Adverbs tell **how**, **when**, or **where** the action takes place.

Examples:
How	When	Where
slowly	yesterday	here
gracefully	today	there
swiftly	tomorrow	everywhere
quickly	soon	

To identify an adverb, locate the verb, then ask yourself if there are any words that tell how, when, or where the action takes place.

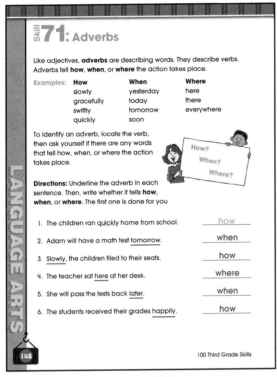

How?
When?
Where?

Directions: Underline the adverb in each sentence. Then, write whether it tells **how**, **when**, or **where**. The first one is done for you

1. The children ran quickly home from school. — how
2. Adam will have a math test tomorrow. — when
3. Slowly, the children filed to their seats. — how
4. The teacher sat here at her desk. — where
5. She will pass the tests back later. — when
6. The students received their grades happily. — how

100 Third Grade Skills
148

Page 149

Skill 71: Adverbs

Directions: Use an **adverb** from the Word Bank to finish each sentence. Make sure the adverb you choose makes sense with the rest of the sentence.

Word Bank			
loudly	here	carefully	carelessly
inside	slowly	below	everywhere

1. Zach left the library book __here__.
2. We looked __everywhere__ for his jacket.
3. We will have recess __inside__ because it is raining.
4. From the top of the mountain, we could see the village far __below__.
5. We watched the turtle move __slowly__ across the yard.
6. Everyone completed the math test __carefully__.
7. The fire was caused by someone __carelessly__ tossing a match.
8. The alarm rang __loudly__ while we were eating.

100 Third Grade Skills
149

Page 150

Skill 72: Articles

A, **an**, and **the** are called **articles**.

A and **an** introduce singular nouns. Use **a** when the next word begins with a consonant sound. Use **an** when the next word begins with a vowel sound.

Examples: **a** chair   **an** antelope

The introduces both singular and plural nouns.

Examples: **the** beaver   **the** flowers

Directions: Underline the correct article for each word.

1. (the, an) field
2. (a, an) award
3. (an, the) ball
4. (a, the) wheels
5. (a, an) inning
6. (an, the) sticks
7. (the, a) goalposts
8. (a, an) obstacle
9. (a, an) umpire
10. (an, the) quarterback
11. (a, an) oven
12. (an, the) oranges
13. (the, a) cities
14. (an, a) elephant
15. (a, the) igloo
16. (a, an) nest
17. (an, a) ape
18. (the, an) staircase
19. (a, the) highways
20. (a, an) yo-yo

100 Third Grade Skills
150

Page 151

Skill 72: Articles

Directions: Write **a** or **an** in each sentence below. The first one is done for you.

1. My bike had __a__ flat tire.
2. They brought __a__ goat to the farm.
3. My mom wears __an__ old pair of shoes to mow the lawn.
4. We had __a__ party for my grandfather.
5. Everybody had __a__ lemonade after the game.
6. We bought __a__ picnic table for our backyard.
7. We saw __a__ cat sleeping in the shade.
8. It was __an__ evening to be remembered.
9. Karina gave __a__ balloon to her brother.
10. It was __an__ amazing day!
11. The park had __an__ old merry-go-round.
12. Our grandpa gave each of us __a__ dollar.

100 Third Grade Skills
151

Answer Key

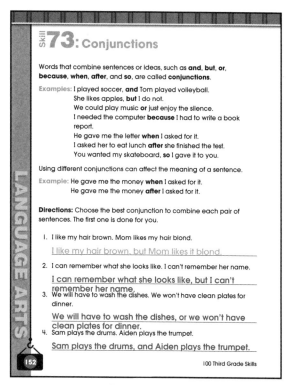

Skill 73: Conjunctions

Words that combine sentences or ideas, such as **and, but, or, because, when, after,** and **so,** are called **conjunctions.**

Examples: I played soccer, **and** Tom played volleyball.
She likes apples, **but** I do not.
We could play music **or** just enjoy the silence.
I needed the computer **because** I had to write a book report.
He gave me the letter **when** I asked for it.
I asked her to eat lunch **after** she finished the test.
You wanted my skateboard, **so** I gave it to you.

Using different conjunctions can affect the meaning of a sentence.

Example: He gave me the money **when** I asked for it.
He gave me the money **after** I asked for it.

Directions: Choose the best conjunction to combine each pair of sentences. The first one is done for you.

1. I like my hair brown. Mom likes my hair blond.

   I like my hair brown, but Mom likes it blond.

2. I can remember what she looks like. I can't remember her name.

   I can remember what she looks like, but I can't remember her name.

3. We will have to wash the dishes. We won't have clean plates for dinner.

   We will have to wash the dishes, or we won't have clean plates for dinner.

4. Sam plays the drums. Aiden plays the trumpet.

   Sam plays the drums, and Aiden plays the trumpet.

152

100 Third Grade Skills

Page 152

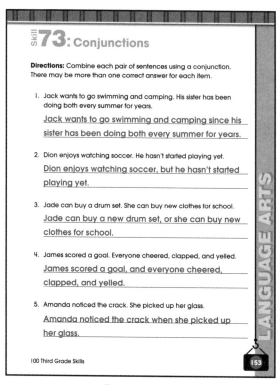

Skill 73: Conjunctions

Directions: Combine each pair of sentences using a conjunction. There may be more than one correct answer for each item.

1. Jack wants to go swimming and camping. His sister has been doing both every summer for years.

   Jack wants to go swimming and camping since his sister has been doing both every summer for years.

2. Dion enjoys watching soccer. He hasn't started playing yet.

   Dion enjoys watching soccer, but he hasn't started playing yet.

3. Jade can buy a drum set. She can buy new clothes for school.

   Jade can buy a new drum set, or she can buy new clothes for school.

4. James scored a goal. Everyone cheered, clapped, and yelled.

   James scored a goal, and everyone cheered, clapped, and yelled.

5. Amanda noticed the crack. She picked up her glass.

   Amanda noticed the crack when she picked up her glass.

100 Third Grade Skills

153

Page 153

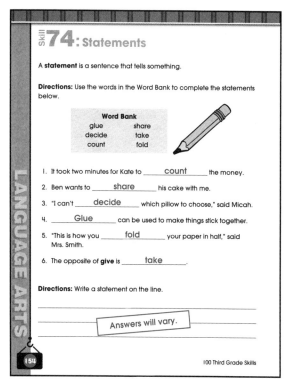

Skill 74: Statements

A **statement** is a sentence that tells something.

Directions: Use the words in the Word Bank to complete the statements below.

Word Bank
glue   share
decide take
count   fold

1. It took two minutes for Kate to _____count_____ the money.

2. Ben wants to _____share_____ his cake with me.

3. "I can't _____decide_____ which pillow to choose," said Micah.

4. _____Glue_____ can be used to make things stick together.

5. "This is how you _____fold_____ your paper in half," said Mrs. Smith.

6. The opposite of **give** is _____take_____.

Directions: Write a statement on the line.

Answers will vary.

154

100 Third Grade Skills

Page 154

Skill 74: Statements

Directions: Read the sentences below. Put an **X** on the line after each sentence that is a statement.

1. It is simple and fun to make your own paint. __X__

2. Buy some ice cream tomorrow. _____

3. We made twenty dollars selling our used books. __X__

4. Stir in the salt until it dissolves. _____

5. Use a juicer to squeeze the oranges. _____

6. We bought napkins and cups. __X__

7. Jessica will be ten in October. __X__

8. Add some ice to your drink. _____

9. Astronauts are planning a mission to Mars. __X__

10. Each muffin contains a teaspoon of sugar. __X__

11. Please have a seat. _____

12. Nobody knew how long the trip would take. __X__

100 Third Grade Skills

155

Page 155

244

Answer Key

Skill 75: Commands

A **command** is a sentence that tells someone to do something.

Directions: Use a word from the Word Bank to finish each command below.

Word Bank

glue   share
decide   enter
add   fold

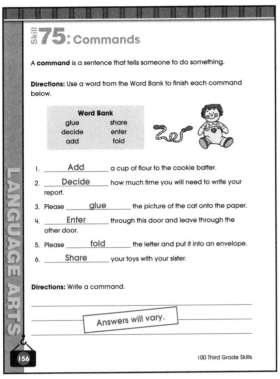

1. _____Add_____ a cup of flour to the cookie batter.
2. _____Decide_____ how much time you will need to write your report.
3. Please _____glue_____ the picture of the cat onto the paper.
4. _____Enter_____ through this door and leave through the other door.
5. Please _____fold_____ the letter and put it into an envelope.
6. _____Share_____ your toys with your sister.

Directions: Write a command.

Answers will vary.

156

100 Third Grade Skills

Page 156

Skill 75: Commands

Directions: Read the sentences below. Put an **X** on the line after each sentence that is a command.

1. Wash your clothes. __X__
2. The refrigerator was full for the party. _____
3. We walked to the park for a picnic. _____
4. Please do not talk so loudly. __X__
5. I had to rewrite my report. _____
6. The movie preview was interesting. _____
7. Don't be late. __X__
8. Sam loves to play in the snow. _____
9. Start your homework before dinner. __X__
10. Nine o'clock is too late to play outside. _____
11. Zip your coat and put on a hat. __X__
12. Our dogs don't like to be inside. _____

100 Third Grade Skills

157

Page 157

Skill 76: Questions

Questions are asking sentences. They begin with a capital letter and end with a question mark. Many questions begin with the words **who**, **what**, **why**, **when**, **where**, or **how**.

Directions: Write six questions using the question words below. Make sure to end each question with a question mark.

1. Who
   _____
2. What
   _____
3. Why
   _____
4. When
   _____   Answers will vary.
5. Where
   _____
6. How
   _____

158

100 Third Grade Skills

Page 158

Skill 76: Questions

Directions: Read the sentences below. Then, rewrite them as questions.

1. The largest frog in the world is called the Goliath frog.
   What is the largest frog in the world?

2. The skin of a toad feels dry and bumpy.
   How does a toad's skin feel?

3. Gliding leaf frogs can glide almost 50 feet in the air.
   How far can gliding leaf frogs glide?

4. The poison dart frog lives in Columbia, South America.
   Where does the poison dart frog live?

5. There are more than 4,000 species of frogs in the world.
   How many species of frogs are there in the world?

100 Third Grade Skills

159

Page 159

Answer Key

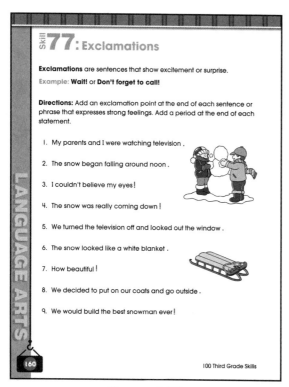

Skill 77: Exclamations

Exclamations are sentences that show excitement or surprise.
Example: Wait! or **Don't forget to call!**

Directions: Add an exclamation point at the end of each sentence or phrase that expresses strong feelings. Add a period at the end of each statement.

1. My parents and I were watching television .
2. The snow began falling around noon .
3. I couldn't believe my eyes !
4. The snow was really coming down !
5. We turned the television off and looked out the window .
6. The snow looked like a white blanket .
7. How beautiful !
8. We decided to put on our coats and go outside .
9. We would build the best snowman ever !

160
100 Third Grade Skills

Page 160

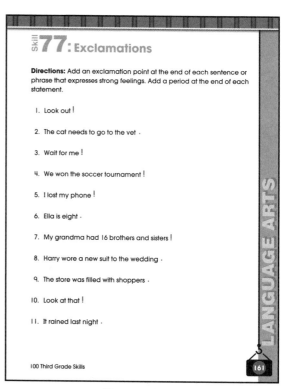

Skill 77: Exclamations

Directions: Add an exclamation point at the end of each sentence or phrase that expresses strong feelings. Add a period at the end of each statement.

1. Look out !
2. The cat needs to go to the vet .
3. Wait for me !
4. We won the soccer tournament !
5. I lost my phone !
6. Ella is eight .
7. My grandma had 16 brothers and sisters !
8. Harry wore a new suit to the wedding .
9. The store was filled with shoppers .
10. Look at that !
11. It rained last night .

100 Third Grade Skills
161

Page 161

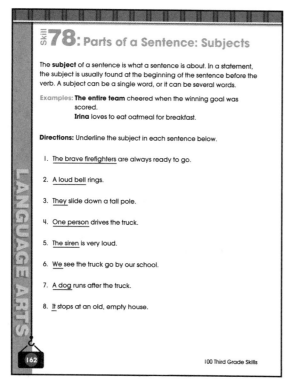

Skill 78: Parts of a Sentence: Subjects

The **subject** of a sentence is what a sentence is about. In a statement, the subject is usually found at the beginning of the sentence before the verb. A subject can be a single word, or it can be several words.

Examples: The entire team cheered when the winning goal was scored.
Irina loves to eat oatmeal for breakfast.

Directions: Underline the subject in each sentence below.

1. The brave firefighters are always ready to go.
2. A loud bell rings.
3. They slide down a tall pole.
4. One person drives the truck.
5. The siren is very loud.
6. We see the truck go by our school.
7. A dog runs after the truck.
8. It stops at an old, empty house.

162
100 Third Grade Skills

Page 162

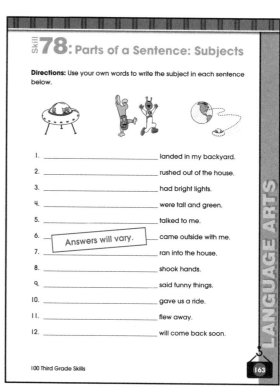

Skill 78: Parts of a Sentence: Subjects

Directions: Use your own words to write the subject in each sentence below.

1. _____ landed in my backyard.
2. _____ rushed out of the house.
3. _____ had bright lights.
4. _____ were tall and green.
5. _____ talked to me.
6. _____ came outside with me.
7. _____ ran into the house.
8. _____ shook hands.
9. _____ said funny things.
10. _____ gave us a ride.
11. _____ flew away.
12. _____ will come back soon.

Answers will vary.

100 Third Grade Skills
163

Page 163

Answer Key

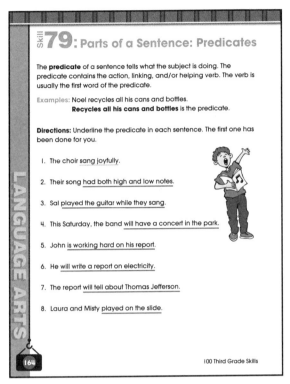

Skill 79: Parts of a Sentence: Predicates

The **predicate** of a sentence tells what the subject is doing. The predicate contains the action, linking, and/or helping verb. The verb is usually the first word of the predicate.

Examples: Noel recycles all his cans and bottles.
Recycles all his cans and bottles is the predicate.

Directions: Underline the predicate in each sentence. The first one has been done for you.

1. The choir sang joyfully.
2. Their song had both high and low notes.
3. Sal played the guitar while they sang.
4. This Saturday, the band will have a concert in the park.
5. John is working hard on his report.
6. He will write a report on electricity.
7. The report will tell about Thomas Jefferson.
8. Laura and Misty played on the slide.

164

100 Third Grade Skills

Page 164

Skill 79: Parts of a Sentence: Predicates

Directions: Write a predicate for each subject to make a complete sentence.

1. The busy mall _____
2. The restaurants _____
3. The children _____ | Answers will vary. |
4. Mom _____
5. The baby _____

Directions: Underline the predicate in each sentence. The first one is done for you.

1. The busy editor wrote a page about subjects and predicates.
2. She was hopeful the children would understand sentences.
3. The children completed their assignment quickly.
4. They went outside.
5. The teacher watched the boys play ball.

100 Third Grade Skills

165

Page 165

Skill 80: Sentence Fragments

A **sentence** is a group of words that expresses a complete thought. It contains a subject and a predicate.

Example: Luna eats tacos every day.

A **sentence fragment** does not express a complete thought. It may be missing either the subject or the predicate.

Example: Lettuce and salsa on it.

Directions: Read each group of words. Circle **S** if it is a sentence. Circle **F** if it is a fragment.

1. Tacos taste delicious.   (S)   F
2. Let the tortillas cool down.   (S)   F
3. Cheese in the refrigerator.   S   (F)
4. Anthony pours salsa on the tortillas.   (S)   F
5. Mom puts the radishes on the tortillas.   (S)   F
6. Sprinkled on top.   S   (F)
7. Everyone eats happily.   (S)   F

166

100 Third Grade Skills

Page 166

Skill 80: Sentence Fragments

Directions: Read each group of words. Circle **S** if it is a sentence. Circle **F** if it is a fragment.

1. Mario sprinkles the tacos with cilantro.   (S)   F
2. More tomatoes.   S   (F)
3. We bake the tacos in the oven for 10 minutes.   (S)   F
4. Served hot.   S   (F)
5. Add avocado.   S   (F)

Directions: Write three sentences of your own about tacos. Each sentence needs a subject and a predicate.

1. _____
   _____
2. _____ | Answers will vary. |
   _____
3. _____
   _____

100 Third Grade Skills

167

Page 167

Answer Key

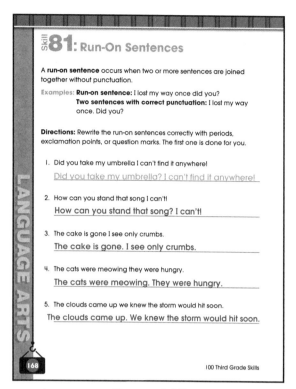

Skill 81: Run-On Sentences

A **run-on sentence** occurs when two or more sentences are joined together without punctuation.

Examples: Run-on sentence: I lost my way once did you?
Two sentences with correct punctuation: I lost my way once. Did you?

Directions: Rewrite the run-on sentences correctly with periods, exclamation points, or question marks. The first one is done for you.

1. Did you take my umbrella I can't find it anywhere!
   Did you take my umbrella? I can't find it anywhere!

2. How can you stand that song I can't!
   How can you stand that song? I can't!

3. The cake is gone I see only crumbs.
   The cake is gone. I see only crumbs.

4. The cats were meowing they were hungry.
   The cats were meowing. They were hungry.

5. The clouds came up we knew the storm would hit soon.
   The clouds came up. We knew the storm would hit soon.

168

100 Third Grade Skills

Page 168

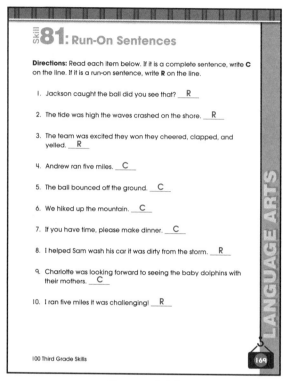

Skill 81: Run-On Sentences

Directions: Read each item below. If it is a complete sentence, write **C** on the line. If it is a run-on sentence, write **R** on the line.

1. Jackson caught the ball did you see that? __R__

2. The tide was high the waves crashed on the shore. __R__

3. The team was excited they won they cheered, clapped, and yelled. __R__

4. Andrew ran five miles. __C__

5. The ball bounced off the ground. __C__

6. We hiked up the mountain. __C__

7. If you have time, please make dinner. __C__

8. I helped Sam wash his car it was dirty from the storm. __R__

9. Charlotte was looking forward to seeing the baby dolphins with their mothers. __C__

10. I ran five miles it was challenging! __R__

100 Third Grade Skills

169

Page 169

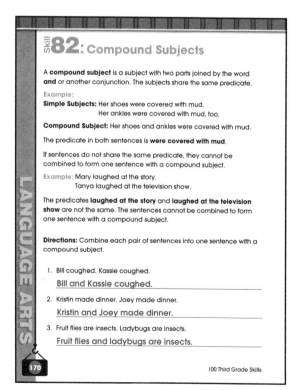

Skill 82: Compound Subjects

A **compound subject** is a subject with two parts joined by the word **and** or another conjunction. The subjects share the same predicate.

Example:
Simple Subjects: Her shoes were covered with mud.
Her ankles were covered with mud, too.
Compound Subject: Her shoes and ankles were covered with mud.

The predicate in both sentences is **were covered with mud.**

If sentences do not share the same predicate, they cannot be combined to form one sentence with a compound subject.

Example: Mary laughed at the story.
Tanya laughed at the television show.

The predicates **laughed at the story** and **laughed at the television show** are not the same. The sentences cannot be combined to form one sentence with a compound subject.

Directions: Combine each pair of sentences into one sentence with a compound subject.

1. Bill coughed. Kassie coughed.
   Bill and Kassie coughed.

2. Kristin made dinner. Joey made dinner.
   Kristin and Joey made dinner.

3. Fruit flies are insects. Ladybugs are insects.
   Fruit flies and ladybugs are insects.

170

100 Third Grade Skills

Page 170

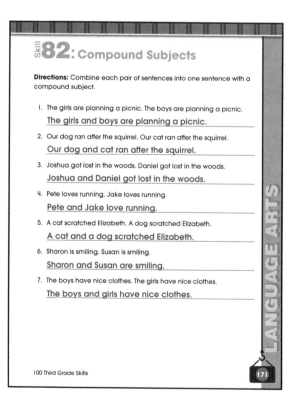

Skill 82: Compound Subjects

Directions: Combine each pair of sentences into one sentence with a compound subject.

1. The girls are planning a picnic. The boys are planning a picnic.
   The girls and boys are planning a picnic.

2. Our dog ran after the squirrel. Our cat ran after the squirrel.
   Our dog and cat ran after the squirrel.

3. Joshua got lost in the woods. Daniel got lost in the woods.
   Joshua and Daniel got lost in the woods.

4. Pete loves running. Jake loves running.
   Pete and Jake love running.

5. A cat scratched Elizabeth. A dog scratched Elizabeth.
   A cat and a dog scratched Elizabeth.

6. Sharon is smiling. Susan is smiling.
   Sharon and Susan are smiling.

7. The boys have nice clothes. The girls have nice clothes.
   The boys and girls have nice clothes.

100 Third Grade Skills

171

Page 171

Answer Key

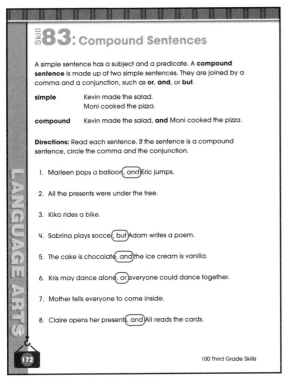

Skill 83: Compound Sentences

A simple sentence has a subject and a predicate. A **compound sentence** is made up of two simple sentences. They are joined by a comma and a conjunction, such as **or**, **and**, or **but**.

simple	Kevin made the salad.
	Moni cooked the pizza.
compound	Kevin made the salad, **and** Moni cooked the pizza.

Directions: Read each sentence. If the sentence is a compound sentence, circle the comma and the conjunction.

1. Marleen pops a balloon⟨, and⟩Eric jumps.

2. All the presents were under the tree.

3. Kiko rides a bike.

4. Sabrina plays soccer⟨, but⟩Adam writes a poem.

5. The cake is chocolate⟨, and⟩the ice cream is vanilla.

6. Kris may dance alone⟨, or⟩everyone could dance together.

7. Mother tells everyone to come inside.

8. Claire opens her presents⟨, and⟩Ali reads the cards.

100 Third Grade Skills

Page 172

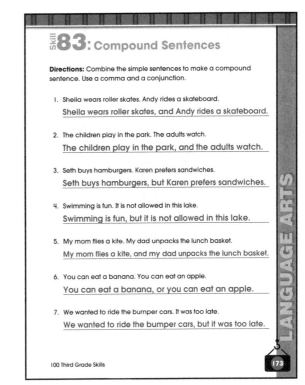

Skill 83: Compound Sentences

Directions: Combine the simple sentences to make a compound sentence. Use a comma and a conjunction.

1. Sheila wears roller skates. Andy rides a skateboard.
   Sheila wears roller skates, and Andy rides a skateboard.

2. The children play in the park. The adults watch.
   The children play in the park, and the adults watch.

3. Seth buys hamburgers. Karen prefers sandwiches.
   Seth buys hamburgers, but Karen prefers sandwiches.

4. Swimming is fun. It is not allowed in this lake.
   Swimming is fun, but it is not allowed in this lake.

5. My mom flies a kite. My dad unpacks the lunch basket.
   My mom flies a kite, and my dad unpacks the lunch basket.

6. You can eat a banana. You can eat an apple.
   You can eat a banana, or you can eat an apple.

7. We wanted to ride the bumper cars. It was too late.
   We wanted to ride the bumper cars, but it was too late.

100 Third Grade Skills

Page 173

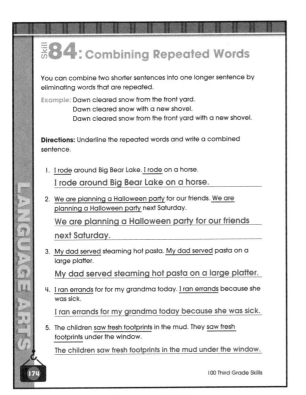

Skill 84: Combining Repeated Words

You can combine two shorter sentences into one longer sentence by eliminating words that are repeated.

Example: Dawn cleared snow from the front yard.
Dawn cleared snow with a new shovel.
Dawn cleared snow from the front yard with a new shovel.

Directions: Underline the repeated words and write a combined sentence.

1. I rode around Big Bear Lake. I rode on a horse.
   I rode around Big Bear Lake on a horse.

2. We are planning a Halloween party for our friends. We are planning a Halloween party next Saturday.
   We are planning a Halloween party for our friends next Saturday.

3. My dad served steaming hot pasta. My dad served pasta on a large platter.
   My dad served steaming hot pasta on a large platter.

4. I ran errands for for my grandma today. I ran errands because she was sick.
   I ran errands for my grandma today because she was sick.

5. The children saw fresh footprints in the mud. They saw fresh footprints under the window.
   The children saw fresh footprints in the mud under the window.

100 Third Grade Skills

Page 174

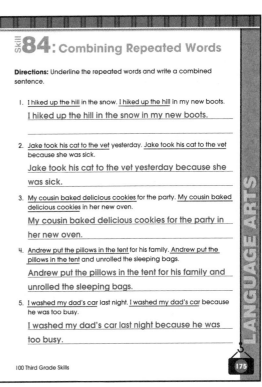

Skill 84: Combining Repeated Words

Directions: Underline the repeated words and write a combined sentence.

1. I hiked up the hill in the snow. I hiked up the hill in my new boots.
   I hiked up the hill in the snow in my new boots.

2. Jake took his cat to the vet yesterday. Jake took his cat to the vet because she was sick.
   Jake took his cat to the vet yesterday because she was sick.

3. My cousin baked delicious cookies for the party. My cousin baked delicious cookies in her new oven.
   My cousin baked delicious cookies for the party in her new oven.

4. Andrew put the pillows in the tent for his family. Andrew put the pillows in the tent and unrolled the sleeping bags.
   Andrew put the pillows in the tent for his family and unrolled the sleeping bags.

5. I washed my dad's car last night. I washed my dad's car because he was too busy.
   I washed my dad's car last night because he was too busy.

100 Third Grade Skills

Page 175

Answer Key

Page 176

Skill 85: Capitalizing the First Word in a Sentence and "I"

The first word in a sentence should begin with a capital letter. The name of a person begins with a capital letter. The pronoun **I** is written as a capital letter.

Directions: Read each sentence. Use three short lines to underline the first letter of each word that needs a capital letter. Rewrite the word correctly. The first one is done for you.

1. ___Today___ today is the first day of school.
2. ___I___ i take the bus to school.
3. ___I___ Jamie and i play soccer at recess.
4. ___I___ everyone has to write a story about something fun they did over the summer.
5. ___I___ i finished my science experiment.
6. ___Lunch___ lunch is served at 11:30.
7. ___Our___ our principal came to visit our class.
8. ___I___ Sam and i were quiet in the library.
9. ___The___ the teacher writes the homework on the board.
10. ___I___ i cleaned my desk before I went home.
11. ___Have___ have a great day.

Page 177

Skill 85: Capitalizing the First Word in a Sentence and "I"

Directions: Read each sentence. Use three short lines to underline the first letter of each word that needs a capital letter. Rewrite each sentence correctly. The first one is done for you.

1. The librarian helped tracy find a book about susan b. anthony.
   The librarian helped Tracy find a book about Susan B. Anthony.

2. i learned that george washington was the first president. *I learned that George Washington was the first president.*

3. matt and i are writing a report about john f. kennedy. *Matt and I are writing a report about John F. Kennedy.*

4. elisa and i are studying about samuel adams. *Elisa and I are studying about Samuel Adams.*

5. harriet tubman helped rescue many people from slavery. *Harriet Tubman helped rescue many people from slavery.*

6. Many people admire helen keller's courage and intelligence. *Many people admire Helen Keller's courage and intelligence.*

7. Can i write a report about jackie robinson? *Can I write a report about Jackie Robinson?*

Page 178

Skill 86: Capitalizing Names and Titles

Capitalize the **specific names of people and pets**.

Examples: My cousin **Peter** moved here from Germany.
We named the kitten **Zorro**.

A **title** that comes before a name is capitalized.

Examples: **Grandpa** Bruce   **President** Abraham Lincoln

Titles of respect are also capitalized.

Examples: **Dr.** Gupta   **Mrs.** Cohen

If a title is not used with a name, it is not capitalized.

Directions: Complete each sentence below with the words in parentheses ( ). Some of the words will need to be capitalized. Others will not.

1. Kelly took her dog, ___Abby___, for a walk to the park. (abby)
2. My school has a new ___teacher___. (teacher)
3. On Saturday, ___Grandpa___ is coming to visit. (grandpa)
4. The best teacher I ever had was ___Mr. Benham___. (mr. benham)
5. The baby panda at the zoo is named ___Mica___. (mica)

Page 179

Skill 86: Capitalizing Names and Titles

Directions: Write the words in the correct column with capital letters at the beginning of each word. Use the words in the word box.

president barack obama		rover
mr. hoffer		uncle brian
grandma stella		spot
judge hommell		dr. kosten
captain albertson		ace

people	people with titles	pets
Grandma Stella	Judge Hommell	Ace
Uncle Brian	Mr. Hoffer	Rover
	President Barack Obama	Spot
	Captain Albertson	
	Dr. Kosten	

Answer Key

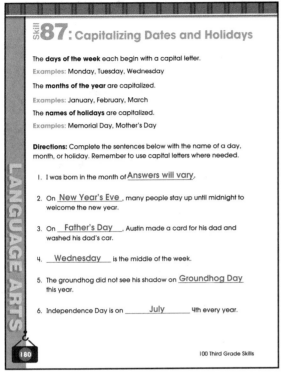

Page 180

Page 181

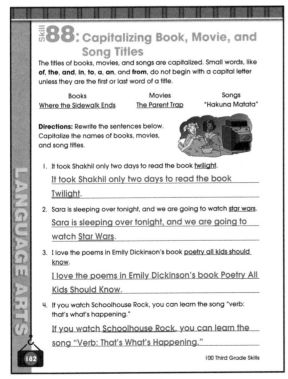

Page 182

Page 183

Answer Key

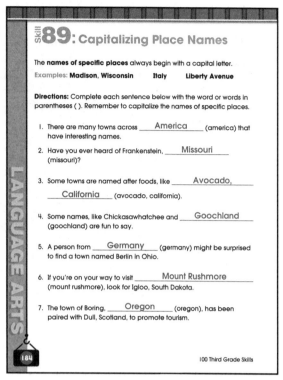

Skill 89: Capitalizing Place Names

The **names of specific places** always begin with a capital letter.

Examples: **Madison, Wisconsin**   **Italy**   **Liberty Avenue**

Directions: Complete each sentence below with the word or words in parentheses ( ). Remember to capitalize the names of specific places.

1. There are many towns across ___America___ (america) that have interesting names.

2. Have you ever heard of Frankenstein, ___Missouri___ (missouri)?

3. Some towns are named after foods, like ___Avocado,___ ___California___ (avocado, california).

4. Some names, like Chickasawhatchee and ___Goochland___ (goochland) are fun to say.

5. A person from ___Germany___ (germany) might be surprised to find a town named Berlin in Ohio.

6. If you're on your way to visit ___Mount Rushmore___ (mount rushmore), look for Igloo, South Dakota.

7. The town of Boring, ___Oregon___ (oregon), has been paired with Dull, Scotland, to promote tourism.

LANGUAGE ARTS

184

100 Third Grade Skills

Page 184

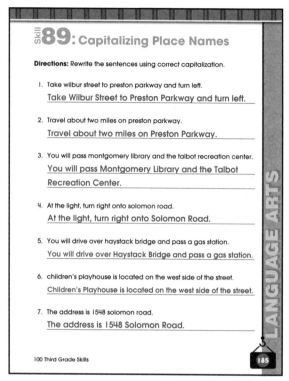

Skill 89: Capitalizing Place Names

Directions: Rewrite the sentences using correct capitalization.

1. Take wilbur street to preston parkway and turn left.
   <u>Take Wilbur Street to Preston Parkway and turn left.</u>

2. Travel about two miles on preston parkway.
   <u>Travel about two miles on Preston Parkway.</u>

3. You will pass montgomery library and the talbot recreation center.
   <u>You will pass Montgomery Library and the Talbot Recreation Center.</u>

4. At the light, turn right onto solomon road.
   <u>At the light, turn right onto Solomon Road.</u>

5. You will drive over haystack bridge and pass a gas station.
   <u>You will drive over Haystack Bridge and pass a gas station.</u>

6. children's playhouse is located on the west side of the street.
   <u>Children's Playhouse is located on the west side of the street.</u>

7. The address is 1548 solomon road.
   <u>The address is 1548 Solomon Road.</u>

LANGUAGE ARTS

100 Third Grade Skills

185

Page 185

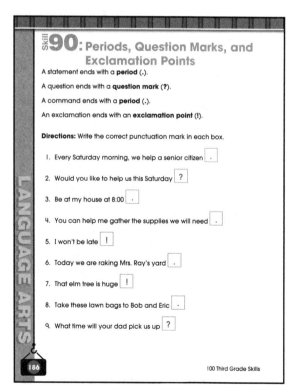

Skill 90: Periods, Question Marks, and Exclamation Points

A statement ends with a **period (.)**.

A question ends with a **question mark (?)**.

A command ends with a **period (.)**.

An exclamation ends with an **exclamation point (!)**.

Directions: Write the correct punctuation mark in each box.

1. Every Saturday morning, we help a senior citizen [.]

2. Would you like to help us this Saturday [?]

3. Be at my house at 8:00 [.]

4. You can help me gather the supplies we will need [.]

5. I won't be late [!]

6. Today we are raking Mrs. Ray's yard [.]

7. That elm tree is huge [!]

8. Take these lawn bags to Bob and Eric [.]

9. What time will your dad pick us up [?]

LANGUAGE ARTS

186

100 Third Grade Skills

Page 186

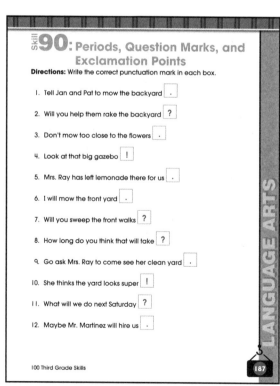

Skill 90: Periods, Question Marks, and Exclamation Points

Directions: Write the correct punctuation mark in each box.

1. Tell Jan and Pat to mow the backyard [.]

2. Will you help them rake the backyard [?]

3. Don't mow too close to the flowers [.]

4. Look at that big gazebo [!]

5. Mrs. Ray has left lemonade there for us [.]

6. I will mow the front yard [.]

7. Will you sweep the front walks [?]

8. How long do you think that will take [?]

9. Go ask Mrs. Ray to come see her clean yard [.]

10. She thinks the yard looks super [!]

11. What will we do next Saturday [?]

12. Maybe Mr. Martinez will hire us [.]

LANGUAGE ARTS

100 Third Grade Skills

187

Page 187

Answer Key

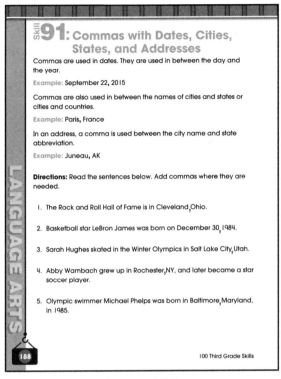

Skill 91: Commas with Dates, Cities, States, and Addresses

Commas are used in dates. They are used in between the day and the year.

Example: September 22, 2015

Commas are also used in between the names of cities and states or cities and countries.

Example: Paris, France

In an address, a comma is used between the city name and state abbreviation.

Example: Juneau, AK

Directions: Read the sentences below. Add commas where they are needed.

1. The Rock and Roll Hall of Fame is in Cleveland, Ohio.
2. Basketball star LeBron James was born on December 30, 1984.
3. Sarah Hughes skated in the Winter Olympics in Salt Lake City, Utah.
4. Abby Wambach grew up in Rochester, NY, and later became a star soccer player.
5. Olympic swimmer Michael Phelps was born in Baltimore, Maryland, in 1985.

188

100 Third Grade Skills

Page 188

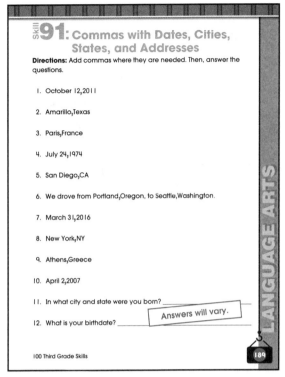

Skill 91: Commas with Dates, Cities, States, and Addresses

Directions: Add commas where they are needed. Then, answer the questions.

1. October 12, 2011
2. Amarillo, Texas
3. Paris, France
4. July 24, 1974
5. San Diego, CA
6. We drove from Portland, Oregon, to Seattle, Washington.
7. March 31, 2016
8. New York, NY
9. Athens, Greece
10. April 2, 2007
11. In what city and state were you born? _____
12. What is your birthdate? _____ Answers will vary.

100 Third Grade Skills

189

Page 189

Skill 92: Commas in a Series

A **series** is a list of words. Use a comma after each word in a series except the last word. Use a conjunction (**and, or**) before the last word in a series.

Examples: My family includes my **mom, dad, sister, and me.**
Fruit, cookies, or popcorn are our snack choices today.

Directions: Add commas to these sentences.

1. We are going on a trip to Germany, Prague, and France.
2. My mother, father, sister and I are packing our suitcases.
3. I need to pack my shampoo, toothpaste, and lotion.
4. Mom, I can't find my shirt, pants, or gloves!
5. I can take my blue jeans, green shorts, and purple socks.
6. Do I need tennis shoes, nice shoes, or boots?
7. A magazine, a book, and music are also good things to pack.
8. Mom tucks me in, kisses me, and tells me good night.
9. Mom turns out the lights in my room, the hall, and the stairs.
10. I can't wait to travel, play, and have fun!

190

100 Third Grade Skills

Page 190

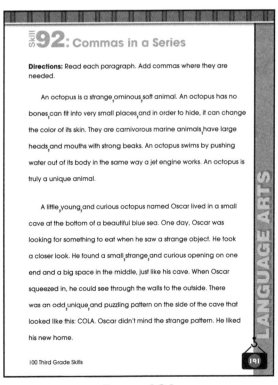

Skill 92: Commas in a Series

Directions: Read each paragraph. Add commas where they are needed.

An octopus is a strange, ominous, soft animal. An octopus has no bones, can fit into very small places, and in order to hide, it can change the color of its skin. They are carnivorous marine animals, have large heads, and mouths with strong beaks. An octopus swims by pushing water out of its body in the same way a jet engine works. An octopus is truly a unique animal.

A little, young, and curious octopus named Oscar lived in a small cave at the bottom of a beautiful blue sea. One day, Oscar was looking for something to eat when he saw a strange object. He took a closer look. He found a small, strange, and curious opening on one end and a big space in the middle, just like his cave. When Oscar squeezed in, he could see through the walls to the outside. There was an odd, unique, and puzzling pattern on the side of the cave that looked like this: COLA. Oscar didn't mind the strange pattern. He liked his new home.

100 Third Grade Skills

191

Page 191

Answer Key

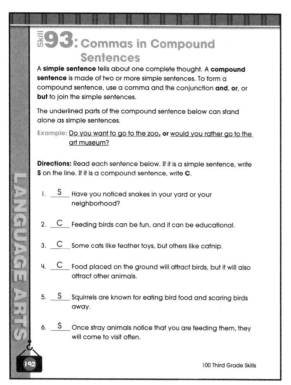

Skill 93: Commas in Compound Sentences

A **simple sentence** tells about one complete thought. A **compound sentence** is made of two or more simple sentences. To form a compound sentence, use a comma and the conjunction **and**, **or**, or **but** to join the simple sentences.

The underlined parts of the compound sentence below can stand alone as simple sentences.

Example: <u>Do you want to go to the zoo</u>, **or** <u>would you rather go to the art museum?</u>

Directions: Read each sentence below. If it is a simple sentence, write **S** on the line. If it is a compound sentence, write **C**.

1. __S__ Have you noticed snakes in your yard or your neighborhood?

2. __C__ Feeding birds can be fun, and it can be educational.

3. __C__ Some cats like feather toys, but others like catnip.

4. __C__ Food placed on the ground will attract birds, but it will also attract other animals.

5. __S__ Squirrels are known for eating bird food and scaring birds away.

6. __S__ Once stray animals notice that you are feeding them, they will come to visit often.

192

100 Third Grade Skills

Page 192

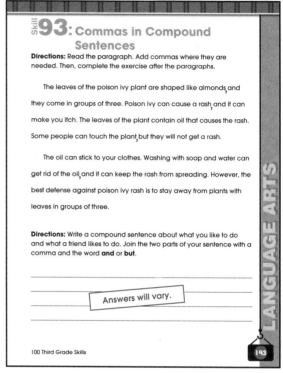

Skill 93: Commas in Compound Sentences

Directions: Read the paragraph. Add commas where they are needed. Then, complete the exercise after the paragraphs.

The leaves of the poison ivy plant are shaped like almonds, and they come in groups of three. Poison ivy can cause a rash, and it can make you itch. The leaves of the plant contain oil that causes the rash. Some people can touch the plant, but they will not get a rash.

The oil can stick to your clothes. Washing with soap and water can get rid of the oil, and it can keep the rash from spreading. However, the best defense against poison ivy rash is to stay away from plants with leaves in groups of three.

Directions: Write a compound sentence about what you like to do and what a friend likes to do. Join the two parts of your sentence with a comma and the word **and** or **but**.

_____

| Answers will vary. |

_____

100 Third Grade Skills

193

Page 193

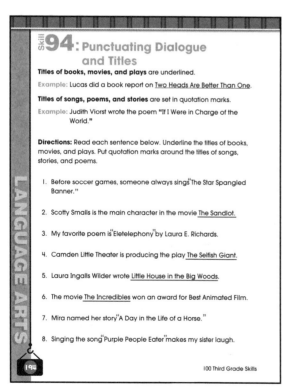

Skill 94: Punctuating Dialogue and Titles

Titles of books, movies, and plays are underlined.

Example: Lucas did a book report on <u>Two Heads Are Better Than One</u>.

Titles of songs, poems, and stories are set in quotation marks.

Example: Judith Viorst wrote the poem "If I Were in Charge of the World."

Directions: Read each sentence below. Underline the titles of books, movies, and plays. Put quotation marks around the titles of songs, stories, and poems.

1. Before soccer games, someone always sings "The Star Spangled Banner."

2. Scotty Smalls is the main character in the movie <u>The Sandlot.</u>

3. My favorite poem is "Eletelephony" by Laura E. Richards.

4. Camden Little Theater is producing the play <u>The Selfish Giant</u>.

5. Laura Ingalls Wilder wrote <u>Little House in the Big Woods</u>.

6. The movie <u>The Incredibles</u> won an award for Best Animated Film.

7. Mira named her story "A Day in the Life of a Horse."

8. Singing the song "Purple People Eater" makes my sister laugh.

194

100 Third Grade Skills

Page 194

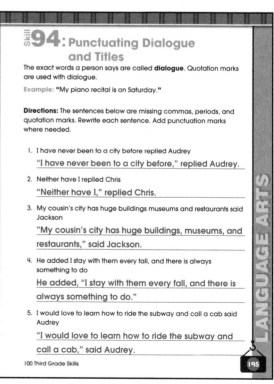

Skill 94: Punctuating Dialogue and Titles

The exact words a person says are called **dialogue**. Quotation marks are used with dialogue.

Example: "My piano recital is on Saturday."

Directions: The sentences below are missing commas, periods, and quotation marks. Rewrite each sentence. Add punctuation marks where needed.

1. I have never been to a city before replied Audrey
   "I have never been to a city before," replied Audrey.

2. Neither have I replied Chris
   "Neither have I," replied Chris.

3. My cousin's city has huge buildings museums and restaurants said Jackson
   "My cousin's city has huge buildings, museums, and restaurants," said Jackson.

4. He added I stay with them every fall, and there is always something to do
   He added, "I stay with them every fall, and there is always something to do."

5. I would love to learn how to ride the subway and call a cab said Audrey
   "I would love to learn how to ride the subway and call a cab," said Audrey.

100 Third Grade Skills

195

Page 195

Answer Key

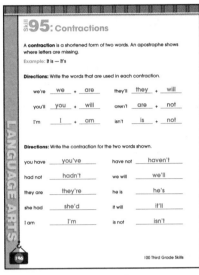

Skill 95: Contractions

A **contraction** is a shortened form of two words. An apostrophe shows where letters are missing.

Example: It is — It's

Directions: Write the words that are used in each contraction.

we're	we + are	they'll	they + will
you'll	you + will	aren't	are + not
I'm	I + am	isn't	is + not

Directions: Write the contraction for the two words shown.

you have	you've	have not	haven't
had not	hadn't	we will	we'll
they are	they're	he is	he's
she had	she'd	it will	it'll
I am	I'm	is not	isn't

100 Third Grade Skills

Page 196

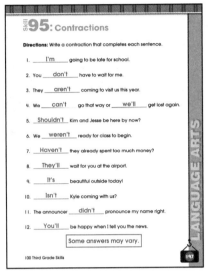

Skill 95: Contractions

Directions: Write a contraction that completes each sentence.

1. __I'm__ going to be late for school.
2. You __don't__ have to wait for me.
3. They __aren't__ coming to visit us this year.
4. We __can't__ go that way or __we'll__ get lost again.
5. __Shouldn't__ Kim and Jesse be here by now?
6. We __weren't__ ready for class to begin.
7. __Haven't__ they already spent too much money?
8. __They'll__ wait for you at the airport.
9. __It's__ beautiful outside today!
10. __Isn't__ Kyle coming with us?
11. The announcer __didn't__ pronounce my name right.
12. __You'll__ be happy when I tell you the news.

Some answers may vary.

100 Third Grade Skills

Page 197

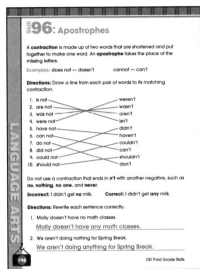

Skill 96: Apostrophes

A **contraction** is made up of two words that are shortened and put together to make one word. An **apostrophe** takes the place of the missing letters.

Examples: does not — doesn't   cannot — can't

Directions: Draw a line from each pair of words to its matching contraction.

1. is not — weren't
2. are not — wasn't
3. was not — aren't
4. were not — isn't
5. have not — didn't
6. can not — haven't
7. do not — couldn't
8. did not — can't
9. could not — shouldn't
10. should not — don't

Do not use a contraction that ends in **n't** with another negative, such as **no, nothing, no one,** and **never.**

Incorrect: I didn't get **no** milk.   **Correct:** I didn't get **any** milk.

Directions: Rewrite each sentence correctly.

1. Molly doesn't have no math classes.
   Molly doesn't have any math classes.
2. We aren't doing nothing for Spring Break.
   We aren't doing anything for Spring Break.

100 Third Grade Skills

Page 198

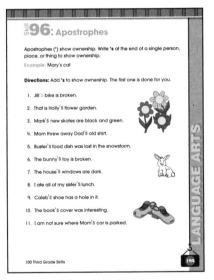

Skill 96: Apostrophes

Apostrophes (') show ownership. Write **'s** at the end of a single person, place, or thing to show ownership.

Example: Mary's cat

Directions: Add **'s** to show ownership. The first one is done for you.

1. Jill's bike is broken.
2. That is Holly's flower garden.
3. Mark's new skates are black and green.
4. Mom threw away Dad's old shirt.
5. Buster's food dish was lost in the snowstorm.
6. The bunny's toy is broken.
7. The house's windows are dark.
8. I ate all of my sister's lunch.
9. Caleb's shoe has a hole in it.
10. The book's cover was interesting.
11. I am not sure where Mom's car is parked.

100 Third Grade Skills

Page 199

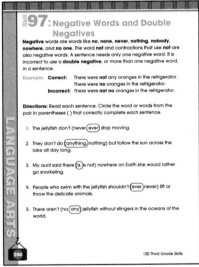

Skill 97: Negative Words and Double Negatives

Negative words are words like **no, none, never, nothing, nobody, nowhere,** and **no one.** The word **not** and contractions that use **not** are also negative words. A sentence needs only one negative word. It is incorrect to use a **double negative,** or more than one negative word, in a sentence.

Example: **Correct:** There were **not** any oranges in the refrigerator.
           There were **no** oranges in the refrigerator.
Incorrect: There were **not no** oranges in the refrigerator.

Directions: Read each sentence. Circle the word or words from the pair in parentheses ( ) that correctly complete each sentence.

1. The jellyfish don't (never, ever) stop moving.
2. They don't do (anything, nothing) but follow the sun across the lake all day long.
3. My aunt said there (is, is not) nowhere on Earth she would rather go snorkeling.
4. People who swim with the jellyfish shouldn't (ever, never) lift or throw the delicate animals.
5. There aren't (no, any) jellyfish without stingers in the oceans of the world.

100 Third Grade Skills

Page 200

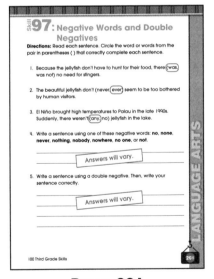

Skill 97: Negative Words and Double Negatives

Directions: Read each sentence. Circle the word or words from the pair in parentheses ( ) that correctly complete each sentence.

1. Because the jellyfish don't have to hunt for their food, there (was, was not) no need for stingers.
2. The beautiful jellyfish don't (never, ever) seem to be too bothered by human visitors.
3. El Niño brought high temperatures to Palau in the late 1990s. Suddenly, there weren't (any, no) jellyfish in the lake.
4. Write a sentence using one of these negative words: **no, none, never, nothing, nobody, nowhere, no one,** or **not.**

   Answers will vary.

5. Write a sentence using a double negative. Then, write your sentence correctly.

   Answers will vary.

100 Third Grade Skills

Page 201

Answer Key

Page 202

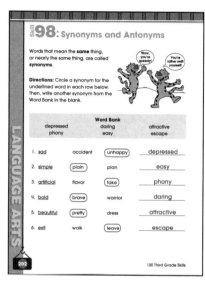

Skill 98: Synonyms and Antonyms

Words that mean the **same** thing, or nearly the same thing, are called **synonyms**.

Directions: Circle a synonym for the underlined word in each row below. Then, write another synonym from the Word Bank in the blank.

Word Bank
| depressed | daring | attractive |
| phony | easy | escape |

1. sad — accident — (unhappy) — depressed
2. simple — (plain) — plan — easy
3. artificial — flavor — (fake) — phony
4. bold — (brave) — warrior — daring
5. beautiful — (pretty) — dress — attractive
6. exit — walk — (leave) — escape

100 Third Grade Skills
202

Page 203

Skill 98: Synonyms and Antonyms

Antonyms are words that are opposites.

Directions: Use the Word Bank to find an antonym for the boldfaced word in each sentence. The first one is done for you.

Word Bank
| open | light | late | hard | slow | old |
| right | full | below | clean | early | neat |

1. My car was **dirty**, but now it is ___clean___.
2. My sister keeps her room **messy**, but I keep mine ___neat___.
3. The sign said, "**Closed**," but the door was ___open___.
4. Is the glass half **empty** or half ___full___?
5. I bought **new** shoes, but I like my ___old___ ones better.
6. Skating is **easy** for me but ___hard___ for my brother.
7. The sky is **dark** at night and ___light___ during the day.
8. Frank is often **tardy**, but Alyssa is usually ___early___.
9. My friend says I am **wrong**, but I say I am ___right___.
10. Jason is a **fast** runner, but Adam is a ___slow___ runner.
11. We were supposed to be **early**, but we were ___late___.

100 Third Grade Skills
203

Page 204

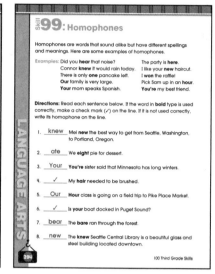

Skill 99: Homophones

Homophones are words that sound alike but have different spellings and meanings. Here are some examples of homophones.

Examples: Did you **hear** that noise? — The party is **here**.
Connor **knew** it would rain today. — I like your **new** haircut.
There is only **one** pancake left. — I **won** the raffle!
Our family is very large. — Pick Sam up in an **hour**.
Your mom speaks Spanish. — **You're** my best friend.

Directions: Read each sentence below. If the word in **bold** type is used correctly, make a check mark (✓) on the line. If it is not used correctly, write its homophone on the line.

1. ___knew___ Mei **new** the best way to get from Seattle, Washington, to Portland, Oregon.
2. ___ate___ We **eight** pie for dessert.
3. ___Your___ **You're** sister said that Minnesota has long winters.
4. ___✓___ My **hair** needed to be brushed.
5. ___Our___ **Hour** class is going on a field trip to Pike Place Market.
6. ___✓___ Is **your** boat docked in Puget Sound?
7. ___bear___ The **bare** ran through the forest.
8. ___new___ The **knew** Seattle Central Library is a beautiful glass and steel building located downtown.

100 Third Grade Skills
204

Page 205

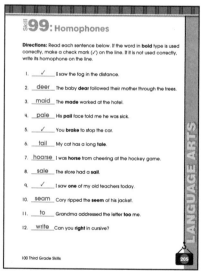

Skill 99: Homophones

Directions: Read each sentence below. If the word in **bold** type is used correctly, make a check mark (✓) on the line. If it is not used correctly, write its homophone on the line.

1. ___✓___ I saw the fog in the distance.
2. ___deer___ The baby **dear** followed their mother through the trees.
3. ___maid___ The **made** worked at the hotel.
4. ___pale___ His **pail** face told me he was sick.
5. ___✓___ You **brake** to stop the car.
6. ___tail___ My cat has a long **tale**.
7. ___hoarse___ I was **horse** from cheering at the hockey game.
8. ___sale___ The store had a **sail**.
9. ___✓___ I saw **one** of my old teachers today.
10. ___seam___ Cory ripped the **seem** of his jacket.
11. ___to___ Grandma addressed the letter **too** me.
12. ___write___ Can you **right** in cursive?

100 Third Grade Skills
205

Page 206

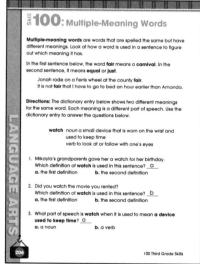

Skill 100: Multiple-Meaning Words

Multiple-meaning words are words that are spelled the same but have different meanings. Look at how a word is used in a sentence to figure out which meaning it has.

In the first sentence below, the word **fair** means a **carnival**. In the second sentence, it means **equal** or **just**.

Jonah rode on a Ferris wheel at the county **fair**.
It is not **fair** that I have to go to bed an hour earlier than Amanda.

Directions: The dictionary entry below shows two different meanings for the same word. Each meaning is a different part of speech. Use the dictionary entry to answer the questions below.

watch *noun* a small device that is worn on the wrist and used to keep time
verb to look at or follow with one's eyes

1. Mikayla's grandparents gave her a watch for her birthday. Which definition of **watch** is used in this sentence? ___a___
a. the first definition   b. the second definition
2. Did you watch the movie you rented? Which definition of **watch** is used in this sentence? ___b___
a. the first definition   b. the second definition
3. What part of speech is **watch** when it is used to mean a **device used to keep time**? ___a___
a. a noun   b. a verb

100 Third Grade Skills
206

Page 207

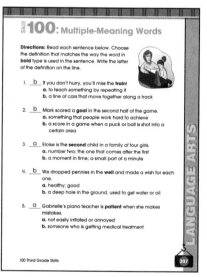

Skill 100: Multiple-Meaning Words

Directions: Read each sentence below. Choose the definition that matches the way the word in **bold** type is used in the sentence. Write the letter of the definition on the line.

1. ___b___ If you don't hurry, you'll miss the **train**!
a. to teach something by repeating it
b. a line of cars that move together along a track
2. ___b___ Mark scored a **goal** in the second half of the game.
a. something that people work hard to achieve
b. a score in a game when a puck or ball is shot into a certain area
3. ___a___ Eloise is the **second** child in a family of four girls.
a. number two; the one that comes after the first
b. a moment in time; a small part of a minute
4. ___b___ We dropped pennies in the **well** and made a wish for each one.
a. healthy; good
b. a deep hole in the ground, used to get water or oil
5. ___a___ Gabrielle's piano teacher is **patient** when she makes mistakes.
a. not easily irritated or annoyed
b. someone who is getting medical treatment

100 Third Grade Skills
207